FRENCH BULLDOG: THE FRENCH BULLDOG BIBLE

From French Bulldog Puppies for Sale,
French Bulldog Breeders, French Bulldog Breeders,
Mini French Bulldogs, Care, Health, Training, & More!

By Susanne Saben

© DYM Worldwide Publishers

DYM Worldwide Publishers

ISBN: 978-1-911355-30-4

Internet. The accuracy and completeness of the information provided herein and opinions stated herein are not guaranteed or warranted to produce any particular results, and the advice or strategies, contained herein may not be suitable for every individual. The author, publisher, distributors, and/or affiliates shall not be liable for any loss incurred as a consequence of the use and application, directly or indirectly of any information presented in this work. This publication is designed to provide information in regards to the subject matter covered. The information included in this book has been compiled to give an overview of the topics covered. The information contained in this book has been compiled to provide an overview of the subject. It is not intended as medical advice and should not be construed as such. For a firm diagnosis of any medical conditions you should consult a doctor or veterinarian (as related to animal health). The writer, publisher, distributors, and/or affiliates of this work are not responsible for any damages or negative consequences following any of the treatments or methods highlighted in this book. Website links are for informational purposes only and should not be seen as a personal endorsement; the same applies to any products or services mentioned in this work. The reader should also be aware that although the web links included were correct at the time of writing they may become out of date in the future. Any pricing or currency exchange rate information was accurate at the time of writing but may become out of date in the future. The Author, Publisher, distributors, and/or affiliates assume no responsibility for pricing and currency exchange rates mentioned within this work.

Table of Contents

French Bulldog Resource List

This quality resource list will help you further maximize your experience with the French Bulldog breed. Enjoy!

Breeders USA (in alphabetical order):

- **Aarn French Bulldogs**
  http://www.aarn-bulldogs.com - USA Breeder, Florida Based, European Stock, Testimonials on Site.
- **All Star French Bulldogs**
  http://www.allstarfrenchbulldogs.com - USA Breeder, all AKC Champion Bloodlines, Many Testimonials, Comprehensive information on site.
- **Aspen French Bulldogs**
  http://www.aspenfrenchbulldogs.com - USA Breeder, Based near Aspen Colorado, Home Raised, AKC Registration.
- **BJ's Frenchies**
  http://www.bjsfrenchies.com - USA Breeder, Based in Iowa, Champion Bloodlines.
- **Big Star French Bulldogs**
  http://www.bigstarbulldogs.com - USA Breeder, Pennsylvania Based, Multiple Champions in the Line, Pedigrees on Site.
- **Bluegrass Frenchies**
  http://www.bluegrassfrenchies.com - USA Breeder, Based in Kentucky, Pedigrees with Over 5 Generations of AKC Champions.

- **Blue Haven French Bulldogs**
  http://www.bluefrenchbulldogscentral.com - USA Breeder, Based in Utah, Family Business.

- **Bon Bon French Bulldogs**
  http://www.bonbonfrenchies.com - USA Breeder, Based in Maryland, Puppies & Stud Service, Pedigrees On Website.

- **Bullworth French Bulldogs**
  http://www.bullworthfrenchbulldogs.com - USA Breeder, Based in Texas, AKC Breeder of Merit.

- **Cherie's Bulldogs**
  http://www.cheriesbulldogs.com - USA Breeder, Based in Atlanta, GA. Good testimonials page on the website and Health Guarantee.

- **Driscol's Blue Gene Frenchies**
  http://www.bluegenefrenchies.com - USA Breeder, Iowa Based, Family Business and Pedigree Information on Website.

- **Forever Young French Bulldogs**
  http://www.foreveryoungfrenchbulldogs.com - USA Breeder, New Jersey / NYC area, Veterinarian Owned.

- **French Bulldogs LA**
  http://www.frenchbulldogsla.com - USA Breeder, based in California. Also an animal behavioural specialist and provides a Health Guarantee.

- **Frenchie Kisses Kennel**
  http://www.frenchiekisseskennel.com - USA Breeder, Based in Washington State, Includes Health Guarantee.

- **Mi Blue Frenchies**
  http://www.mibluefrenchies.com - USA Breeder, Based in Michigan, ABKC (American Bully Kennel Club), DNA Tested.

- **Must Be Frenchies**
  http://www.mustbefrenchies.com - USA Breeder, Based In Missouri, Sire and Dame Info on Website.

- **Poetic French Bulldogs**
  http://www.poeticfrenchbulldogs.com - USA Breeder, Based in Florida, Many Variations Including Blue.

- **Silverblood Frenchies**
  http://www.blue-frenchbulldog.com - USA Breeder, Based in Ft. Lauderdale, FL, Pedigree Information on Site.

- **Smokey Valley Kennel**
  http://www.smokeyvalleyfrenchbulldog.com - USA Breeder, Based in Washington State, French Bulldog Breeder and Show Award winner since the 1980s.

- **Umqua Valley Kennels**
  http://www.frenchbulldog-puppies.net - USA Breeder, Based in Oregon, A lot of useful resources on the site.

- **World of Frenchies**
  http://www.worldoffrenchies.com - USA Breeder, Based in Miami FL. AKC and Pedigreed Bloodlines.

BREEDERS CANADA:

- **Paris Moon Kennel**
  http://www.parismoonkennel.ca - Canada Breeder, Based in Calgary AB.

- **West Coast Rare Bulldogs**
  http://www.westcoastrarebulldogs.com - Canada Breeder, based in Vancouver, British Columbia,

BREEDERS UK:

- **True Blue French Bulldogs**
  http://www.truebluefrenchbulldogs.co.uk/ - UK Breeders, Multiple Champions in the Line, Testimonials on Site.

- **Zandaplatz French Bulldogs**
  http://www.zandaplatz.co.uk - UK Breeders, Credentials and Comprehensive Info on Site.

BREED SPECIFIC & OTHER FURTHER RESOURCES:

AKC: Most Popular Dog Breeds in America & French Bulldog Breed Standards
http://www.akc.org/ American Kennel Club.

Chewy.com
http://www.chewy.com - USA Site, Great selection of extremely tough chew toys, search "Kong" brand for your French Bulldog on the site.

French Bull Dog Club of America
http://www.fbdca.org, Many good resources on the site.

French Bulldog Club of Central Canada
http://frenchbulldogclubofcentralcanada.com/

French Bulldog Club of England
http://www.frenchbulldogclubofengland.org.uk
- Founded 1902.

French Bulldogs Fanciers of Southern California
http://www.frenchiesfirst.com/

French Bulldog Club of Victoria (Australia)
http://www.frenchbulldogclubofvictoria.com.au

Heartland French Bulldog Club

http://www.heartlandfrenchbulldogclub.org

JeffersPet.com

http://www.jefferspet.com

- Extensive Tough Toys and other Supplies, look for Kong brand.

London French Bulldog Meetup Group

(London, England) | Meetup –

https://www.meetup.com/londonfrenchies

Midland & Northern Counties (UK) French Bulldog Club

http://www.mncfrenchbulldogclub.co.uk/

Northern California French Bulldog Club

http://www.ncfbc.com/

Westpawdesign.com - http://www.westpaw.com

- Check out the extremely tough "Tux" toys for your French Bulldog.

Introduction to the French Bulldog Bible

Isn't a Frenchie a really cute dog?

Have you always wanted to own a dog? Has something drawn you to the French Bulldog?

If yes, we all know that it is a somewhat daunting decision. It could be compared to having your own child as you have to deal with feeding, cleaning, and training your dog.

It is a big decision.

If you have been thinking of bringing home a French bulldog, then I guess you cannot resist those cute bat ears and shiny button eyes. It is as if you melt whenever you look at it because it is just too adorable. Its petite build is also irresistible that you want to just bring it home and take care of it! As friendly as it looks, bet you just want to pet a Frenchie.

If you have been thinking of going home to a little fellow that looks like it is always in a good mood, your best bet is a Frenchie. Frenchies are cute and easy-to-deal-with bulldog breeds. Despite their gloomy face, Frenchies are lively, amiable, and dependable.

French bulldogs were first seen in the 1800s from a cross between its bulldog ancestors from England and local ratters from France. Back then, they were already cute and adorable, and it looks like nothing has changed.

French bulldogs are wonderful companion dogs. Their easy-going attitude and tolerance make them good companions for children. They are also very social, so it is not so much of a problem to bring them to public places. They seem to be very active and alert. They are also good watchdogs as they tend to be protective of their owners. They will bark at you if they do not know you!

Taking care of a Frenchie has its own set of challenges. If you have been thinking for so long about the steps to finding a good Frenchie breed, bulldog-proofing your home, and training them, then you should read on.

Dogs love the outdoors. Frenchies are not an exception
(on occasion) but prefer to live inside!

This book will teach you how about the history and the standards of raising a French bulldog. Succeeding chapters will give you tips on how to pick a good breeder or an adoption center, choose between a puppy and an adult Frenchie, pick the right supplies before you bring home your new pet, and prepare your home to your new companion, just to name a few.

CHAPTER 1

French Bulldog History

Just look at those eyes!

Those mesmerising big button eyes are so irresistible; it seems like any Frenchie can enslave a human with a single glance. Those bat ears and a coat so velvety and warm will make you want to pet them.

🐾 17

French bulldogs came all the way from their ancestors that travelled from England to Paris. They came from a line of English bulldogs and Parisian local ratters. That gave them their physical characteristics: they still look like a bulldog, but they have bat ears and are petite in structure.

In this chapter, you will learn more about how French bulldogs came to be. Chapter 1 also talks about the differences among other famous bulldog breeds like the American and the English bulldogs. You will learn their differences in physical appearance and temperament.

History of French Bulldogs

Regardless of their sizes and ages, Frenchies are adorable.

Have you ever wanted a French bulldog? Or have you always been fascinated by its cute face and tiny bone structure?

If yes, you should read on. Perhaps you are wondering why they are called French bulldogs. French bulldogs, also known by the name Frenchies, descended from a miniature molossoid (mastiff) breed. This is a breed of solid, stocky dogs that are believed to have descended from Molossus, a shepherd dog that appeared in Molossia in northwest Greece. Other molossoid breeds include the Neopolitan Mastiff, Cane Corso, Tosa Inu, and Dogo Argentino.

In particular, the Frenchies' origins can be traced as far as the 1800s when their bulldog ancestors from England crossbred with local ratters in Paris, France.

In 1835, blood sports were banned in England, halting the local bull-baiting industry. Since the ancestor English bulldogs no longer served their sporting purpose, they were bred to be 'companions'. Given their huge size, they were crossed with other breeds to make them look friendlier. Eventually, toy bulldogs became more common in England. When the lace industry moved to France, lace makers brought their bulldogs with them. As smaller dogs became more popular, importing small bulldogs became a business in France. From then on, French bulldogs caught on.

In the early days of breeding, Frenchies would have either bat or rose ears. While many preferred the rose ears, the Americans didn't. For them, bat ears are a distinct feature and should be kept for Frenchies. Eventually, the breed lost the rose ears.

The controversy led to the formation of the French Bulldog Club of America, the first organisation in the world devoted to the breed. In 1898, the club sponsored a specialty show in the ballroom of Waldorf-Astoria in New York City to showcase the breed. Since then, Frenchies got wider press coverage, and in 1913, they entered the Westminster Kennel Club. The rest is history.

'I love autumn—lots of leaves I can play with!'

Frenchies are of small stature, but they are solid in terms of weight and height. Ideally, male Frenchies weigh around 31 pounds / 14 kilograms (kg) while bitches are around 26 pounds / 12 kg. They stand at around 18 in / 48 cm – 22 in / 56 cm in height. They may look fragile given their tiny appearance, but Frenchies have a strong bone structure. They can hardly break bones or injure themselves as they have good ligament strength.

Apart from its size, another distinctive feature of a Frenchie is its bat ears and half-domed and half-flat skull. It also has round eyes, a short tail, and a wrinkly face, which makes it look adorable.

Because of their small face, most Frenchies snort, wheeze, and snore loudly. On the plus side, they do not bark much.

They are also generally polite with other people and are very easy to train.

While they were primarily bred as pets and companions, Frenchies are generally intelligent and are good watchdogs.

According to the American Kennel Club, they are often described as a 'clown in the cloak of a philosopher'. They are active and alert but not necessarily boisterous.

Comparing French and English Bulldogs

The bulldog family, (from left to right) English Bulldog & French Bulldog, with a Doberman Pinscher.

There are many different breeds of bulldogs. The most popular ones are the American, English, and French bulldogs. Bulldogs originated from Asiatic mastiffs and were initially used in sports, particularly in bull-baiting arenas.

Generally, bulldogs have large heads, undershot jaw, shorted muzzles, and a strong build. They may appear glum given their features but are mostly softies—gentle and patient.

Apart from the country of origin, French and British bulldogs differ in terms of size and temperaments.

Characteristic	French Bulldog	English Bulldog
Size	Petite	Medium
Colours	Brindle, cream, brindle and white, tan, fawn, black brindle, and white	Fawn and white, brindle and white, red and white, red, grey brindle, and fawn
Temperament	Lively, playful, alert, tolerant, and flexible	Submissive, friendly, social, and determined
Origin	France and England	England

The English bulldog is widely known as the classic bulldog. It may be called just 'bulldog' according to the American Kennel Club. It also used to be called British bulldog.

English bulldogs stand at a medium height. They are very strong looking and have a wide stance. Usually, they weigh around 50 to 60 pounds and look compact, but they may also weigh as much as 40 to 70 pounds (18 to 31 kilograms).

In terms of appearance, bulldogs also have wrinkly faces. Most of the time, they have a flat face. But due to poor breeding, some of them have a slight muzzle.

In terms of colour, French bulldogs come in a variety: brindle, cream, brindle and white, tan, fawn, black brindle, and white. English bulldogs, on the other hand, be fawn and white, brindle and white, red and white, red, grey brindle, and fawn. If they are not purebred, they will not have a red nose.

In terms of temperament, bulldogs look intimidating, but are actually gentle, and like being given attention. They are also protective of their owners, which make them excellent watchdogs. Apart from that, they are quite persistent.

The main difference between an English and a French bulldog is its disposition. English bulldogs are generally more submissive to their owners. They are friendly as well as determined. Meanwhile, Frenchies are characterised by their liveliness. They are alert and playful. They also easily adapt to their surroundings and are very tolerant.

'What's that noise?'

Frenchies are known to be amiable petite dogs. They rarely bark and remain patient and calm with their owners. English bulldogs are also patient and amiable and can easily connect with kids. However, they may become too sensitive at times and may get highly attached to their owners to the point that they are hesitant to go out of the house without them.

In terms of health issues, French bulldogs seem to have fewer and thus live longer than English bulldogs. Frenchies usually live around 9 to 11 years while bulldogs can stay around 8 to 10 years.

If drooling is an issue for you, English bulldogs are known to have a higher drooling tendency compared to Frenchies.

Comparing French and American Bulldogs

As mentioned earlier, the American bulldog is another popular bulldog breed.

American bulldogs are the largest among the three. They are athletic and agile dogs. Compared to the other two, this breed has the longest legs. They are not only loyal and reliable, but they are also brave and determined. They are generally protective of their owner and love doing acts of heroism toward them.

Known for their alpha characteristics, male American bulldogs are stockier and heavier boned than their female counterparts. Their square-shaped heads are also larger with very strong jaws while the necks are muscular. Their nose is black, red, brown or grizzle, although black is the preferred colour based on the standard. These bulldogs come in different colours such as red brindle, white, red, brown, tan, fawn, and piebald.

Known to be giants, American bulldogs can stand as high as 20 to 27 inches / 51cm to 68cm and can weigh as much as 70 to 120 pounds / 31kg to 54kg.

Characteristic	French Bulldog	American Bulldog
Size	Petite	Large
Colours	Brindle, cream, brindle and white, tan, fawn, black brindle, and white	Red brindle, white, red, brown, tan, fawn, and piebald
Temperament	Lively, playful, alert, tolerant, and flexible	Athletic, agile, affectionate, courageous, energetic, and social
Origin	France and England	United States of America

Generally, both French and American bulldogs are easy to maintain. Both are fit for owners who do not want to spend much time and money on their dogs.

The main difference between the two, apart from their origin and size, is their exercise needs and temperament.

In terms of temperament, American bulldogs are very affectionate. They are alert and courageous, which make them good watchdogs. Similar to Frenchies, they will bark when an intruder is present.

Known to be the most athletic of the three, American bulldogs need to exercise regularly. They should be taken on a long walk daily. They are the perfect companion for owners who enjoy fitness activities.

American bulldogs participate in a wide range of activities such as guarding, Schutzhund or Internationale Prüfungs-Ordnung (protection training), tracking, hunting, and weight pulling. American bulldogs are classified as a working class as opposed to Frenchies, which are non-sporting.

It is also easier to train American bulldogs than Frenchies. They are great for first-time dog owners as they obey and listen well quickly. Compared to French bulldogs, American bulldogs can be stubborn, so owners may have to ask help from obedience schools in training them.

In terms of life expectancy, American bulldogs tend to live longer than Frenchies. They can outlive them for about 2 to 3 years, giving them a life expectancy of 11 to 14 years. However, they are prone to hip dysplasia.

While American bulldogs tend to be more agile than Frenchies, the upside of having French bulldogs is that they adapt better to new environments.

In terms of shedding, American bulldogs tend to shed more than Frenchies, which shed only seasonally.

CHAPTER 2

French Bulldogs Traits: What Should I Look For?

Frenchies in different colours: (from left to right) pied, fawn, and brindle.

I f you have finally made up your mind that you want a Frenchie over other bulldogs, then you should read on to know about spotting a purebred French bulldog.

For beginners, the colour of the coat should be a giveaway as there are only three French bulldog colours recognised by different kennel clubs around the world: brindle, fawn, and pied. Other colours (black, tan, and blue) may not be recognised by the standard, but still remain among owners' favorites.

This chapter will also tell you about Frenchies' temperament. To give you an idea, French bulldogs are widely known to be great companions. They are very friendly! However, they can be stubborn at times, which gives you, the owner, a bit of a hard time training them.

How to Spot a Purebred French Bulldog

A French bulldog thanks its good fortune—it got an amazing meal!

Why should you go for a purebred French bulldog? For those who want to be sure about your dog's size and health, you are advised to go for a purebred dog. Specifically, if you want a small, sensitive, and sometimes stubborn dog that does not bark so much, then you should opt for a purebred French bulldog.

Do not be fooled by its glum expression. This breed of puppies is friendly and entertaining. Since the French bulldog is a rare dog breed, you should be wary of scammers who want to fool you into buying something else other than this breed.

Here are ways to avoid being scammed when trying to get a purebred French bulldog:

1. Do your research.

Before adopting a French bulldog, you should know the salient physical qualities to look out for. Read about French bulldogs and understand what sets them apart from other companion dogs. Knowing how they usually look and behave is a step away from being deceived by scammers.

Doing your research will also arm you with the proper questions you should be asking breeders about the French bulldogs. Remember that French bulldogs are small, unlike most other bulldogs that are of medium size. They also have a short back unlike the dachshund.

2. Know how to spot a French bulldog.

Would you know how to spot a French bulldog from a litter of pugs, bulldogs, and Boston terriers? If you do not want to be misled by scammers into adopting other dogs, it is best that you master the salient physical features that define French bulldogs.

Remember that this breed sports a flat and wrinkled muzzle. If you're adopting an adult French bulldog, you should also notice they are lean yet muscular.

This companion dog also has a very dense mass—one of the reasons why they are not good swimmers. French bulldogs that weigh more than 28 pounds (12 kilograms) are not up to standard, according to the American Kennel Club. Unlike that of the Boston terriers, the tail of French bulldogs is never docked. Their ears are not cropped.

3. Find a reputable breeder.

Make sure you buy from a reputable breeder. How can you differentiate reputable from the shady ones?

Remember that trustworthy breeders have nothing to fear, so they will likely share all the needed information about their dogs, including the photos, pedigrees, and health records. A reputable breeder also should have available tests for the health of their dogs. Not only will a reputable breeder not fool you, but he can also give you pro tips on how to grow a French bulldog.

Finding a reputable French bulldog breeder will also be tackled in-depth in a separate chapter.

4. Be wary of breeders selling French bulldogs at a low price.

Remember that purebred French bulldogs can be quite expensive. If the price is too cheap to be true, then that can be a red flag. With an average cost of $700 (£565), raising and taking care of French bulldogs can be expensive.

Recognised French Bulldog Colours: Brindle French Bulldog, Fawn French Bulldog, and Pied French Bulldog

Imagine yourself as a prospective dog owner. How would you want your French bulldog to look like?

One of the good things about the breed of French bulldogs is that they come in an array of colours and patterns. On the flipside, having so many options to choose from sometimes makes it hard for prospective dog owners to decide on what kind of French bulldog to adopt.

Before going into the details of the different recognised French bulldog colours, you should familiarise yourself of the different kennel clubs that exist in the world. Kennel clubs are the official registry of purebred dog pedigrees, and they divide dog pedigrees into different classes. Under the American Kennel Club and the Canadian Kennel Club, the French bulldog is categorised under the non-sporting group breed. The Fédération Cynologique Internationale, on the other hand, categorised the French bulldog as a molossian-type dog.

The registries have also set standards for each particular breed. Under American Kennel Club (AKC), this is indicated through the 'official breed standard'. Any form of departure on the dog's physical feature is considered a disqualification to these standards.

Here are the different French bulldog colours:

Brindle

Brindle, the most dominant colour pattern among French bulldogs, is a coat colouring pattern that appears in dogs, guinea pigs, and cattle. It is characterised by streaks of colour that are irregular and usually a few shades darker than the base coat.

Standard brindle French bulldogs usually have a predominantly black coat, punctuated by lighter-coloured hairs mixed in it. In some dogs with seal brindle, the lighter-coloured hairs may seem invisible at first inspection but a closer look will reveal the light-coloured hair quietly tucked beneath the dog's coat. In some cases, the lighter hairs appear more prominent than the dog's coat, resulting in a reverse brindle.

Fawn

Fawn French bulldogs come in different shades of brown from cream to caramel or a light tan to a dark reddish-brown colour. Brindle French bulldogs are more dominant than the fawn. This means that a dog must inherit a copy of the fawn gene (Ky) from both its parents, to be truly considered fawn.

Don't be mistaken, though. Contrary to what most people assume, fawn French bulldogs do not come in a completely uniform colour. The tint of its back, sides, head, and ears is usually darker than the rest of its lower body and legs.

Pied

French bulldogs also appear in white or eggshell-coloured coating with one or more patches of darker colour. Frenchies who exhibit this kind of appearance fall into the last category of French bulldogs: pied.

Pied is the least recessive trait among the three. The size, number, shade, and area of the patch vary from one pied to another, making this particular type of French bulldog unique. Some pieds have a dominant coating of white or eggshell with only a small patch or patches of darker colour. In some cases, the darker patches are more dominant than the dog's white coat. Some patches also appear on the dog's tail or around its eye.

In order for a pup to come out as pied, it should inherit the recessive trait of piedness both from its mother and father.

Other French Bulldog Colours: Black, Tan, and Blue French Bulldog

The previous chapter discussed the three colour patterns of French bulldogs recognised by different kennel clubs around the world.

This next chapter of the book is dedicated to the other colours of French bulldogs that are not recognised by the kennel clubs around the world. Specifically, this chapter will tackle the black, tan, and blue colours of the French bulldog. Despite not being recognised by kennel clubs, these colours and patterns have been proven a favorite among dog owners.

French bulldogs that come in black, tan, and blue are no different from dogs that exhibit brindle, fawn, or pied colour patterns. Just like them, grooming the fur of the black, blue, and tan Frenchies is manageable, only requiring a bristle brush at least once a week.

Why are there 'rare' French bulldog colours? The different colours and patterns that are in French bulldogs are essentially based on and dependent on their genes. Genes, as taught in our biology classes, are classified into two inheritance patterns: dominant and recessive. For a puppy to exhibit a recessive gene, both its mother and father should be able to pass on the recessive gene to its offspring. Otherwise, in a case where a pup inherits both dominant and recessive genes from each of its parents, the pup will surely express the dominant gene.

To be able to understand why certain French bulldogs appear as they are, it is important to keep in mind how genes work. Essentially, the rarity of a French bulldog's colour and pattern usually influences its pricing in the market.

Before we get lost in the quick biology lesson on genes, here's a rundown of what you need to know about French bulldogs that come in the beautiful colours of black, blue, and tan.

French bulldogs that come in pure black with no brindling or streaks of lighter-coloured hair have a recessive black gene. Some black French bulldogs come with tan points. This is created by another recessive gene, and in some instances, this form can appear as pure blue with tan streaks. Black French bulldogs are not recognised by various kennel clubs partly because many of the standards set by these organisations are outdated.

Like black French bulldogs, tan Frenchies are a result of a recessive gene that is passed on by both its parents. This recessive, while naturally occurring, is very rare in this dog breed. Some tan French bulldogs are paired with other colours such as black, blue, and chocolate. In other dog breeds like Dobermans and Rottweilers, tan is a common and dominant pattern.

The rarest French bulldog is that which comes in the form of blue. In some cases, French bulldogs have stunning blue brindles. French bulldogs that exhibit the blue brindle pattern inherited d, or dilute, genes from both their mother and father. The dilute gene causes the supposedly black hair to turn into the rare and equally gorgeous colour of blue grey.

Understanding the French Bulldog and Its Temperament

Considering the temperament of the French bulldog, is it the best dog breed for you and your family?

Many people see dogs in the same light: a domesticated canine that serves as a perfect pet. But dog breeders and owners know better: different dog breeds exhibit distinct characteristics that may not be present in others. In other words, all dogs are not the same!

In choosing a pet, it's considered a rule of thumb to consider not only the potential pet's outward appearance but also its manner and characteristics. So, before making the jump of adopting a French bulldog, make sure that its temperament and defining characteristics perfectly match your own personality!

Here are a few things you need to know about the French bulldog:

French bulldogs are fun and loving.

Never be fooled by the French bulldogs' glum expression. In truth, they are playful and very affectionate dogs. They are so affectionate that they usually crave lots of attention from their owners. Being deprived of attention and human interaction will result to a psychological let-down for the French bulldogs. This very lovable breed also mixes well with other dog breeds including young ones!

Given their small and stocky frame, French bulldogs also make cuddly companions. Unlike their American counterparts, French bulldogs do not grow into a massive frame even when they reach adulthood, making them perfect for hugging.

French bulldogs do not do well in extreme cold or heat.

French bulldogs crave for the Goldilocks kind of weather: not too cold, not too warm—just right.

With their single short coat coupled with their compromised breathing system, the French bulldogs find it challenging to efficiently regulate their temperature. Essentially, this means that Frenchies shiver easily in the cold. French bulldogs require extra warm clothing during winter or when in a cold living area.

Their indisposition for the cold, however, does not make them comfortable in a very warm weather. French bulldog owners should take the necessary precautions during hot or humid weather. Avoid letting your French bulldogs suffer from a heat stroke by making sure they have access to air-conditioning especially when they live indoors.

French bulldogs are quiet.

Looking for a quiet pet? French bulldogs are the right match for you. They have a sensible attitude toward barking, only doing so when they want to draw attention. They also have a very calm nature. This is the reason why those who reside in apartments or condominiums choose French bulldogs for their pet.

French bulldogs are reluctant learners.

Be warned: French bulldogs are not suitable for impatient dog owners. One negative, but most of the time tolerable, characteristic of the French bulldogs is their stubbornness. Massive patience and persistence are the secrets to effectively training them. If you want your French bulldog to learn some basic tricks, you have to use short signals and develop a consistent habit. Otherwise, you may have to settle for a dog that is not well trained, compared to other companion pets.

CHAPTER 3

Bringing a French Bulldog Puppy Into Your Life, What Should I Be Aware Of?

Photo 10. 'Yes, I can be your best buddy,' says the French bulldog puppy.

After knowing the basics about a French bulldog, you need to know how well it will fit in your life—the way you live, your family, and your home, among others. Owning a dog is a responsibility. You cannot just buy one and then give it up once you find it difficult to integrate into your life. That kind of thinking is the primary reason why they are a lot of dogs in adoption shelters.

This chapter gives a more in-depth discussion on the temperament and characteristics of Frenchies. Are they good for children? Are they aggressive toward other people or other dogs or animals? Questions like 'Why are they so small?' or 'Do they have serious health issues?' will be answered in this chapter.

Is the French Bulldog a Good Fit for You or Your Family?

The French bulldog breed is easily becoming a favourite choice by many as their companion or pet. This does not come as a surprise given how lovable and cuddly Frenchies are, especially compared to their American cousins.

Despite how easy-going Frenchies are, they are not meant for everyone. How will you then know if the French bulldog is a right match for you and your family?

Making the decision of acquiring a French bulldog, just like any pet, should be taken seriously.

There are many ways to check if a French bulldog is a right fit for you and your family. All you have to do is to consider your own lifestyle, schedule, and capacity to take care of it and check if they match with the usual demands of a French bulldog.

You have the luxury of time.

Like what was said in the earlier part of this book, French bulldogs are attention seekers. They need the constant affirmation that they are loved by their dog owners. If you or your family members are not the busy types, then a French bulldog will not have a hard time seeking for love and tender care from you.

In any case, being busy and having a hectic schedule is not necessarily an automatic deterrent to acquiring a French bulldog. You may opt to plan a schedule where you and other family members can take turns in taking care of your pet. You can divide the time of the day among yourselves. This way, you will be able to keep a French bulldog without overhauling your lifestyle.

You are patient.

Unlike golden retrievers and other dog breeds that are fast learners, French bulldogs are reluctant learners. Teaching French bulldogs the basic lessons may take longer than usual because they can be stubborn. This is why French bulldogs are best paired with patient dog owners.

To develop an effective house training, you will have to make the training a habit and use simple signals and instructions. Are you up for this challenge? If you don't think you can handle a consistent training schedule for your dog or doubt that you are patient enough to match the usual stubbornness of French bulldogs, then be ready to maximise the use of your cleaning tools to compensate for this.

An alternative is to hire a professional dog trainer to make sure your dog gets the needed house training.

You are not into outdoor activities.

Because of their compromised breathing system and small structure, French bulldogs are limited in the outdoor activities that they can handle. They also sleep a lot. And by a lot, it means you can expect them lying around the house almost the entire day. Because they are dense, they are also not particularly the best swimmers.

Is Your Home Suitable for a French Bulldog?

Adopting or purchasing a dog should not be taken lightly. Like choosing your college course or career path, getting a dog is an important life commitment as much as it is a responsibility.

There are a few questions that you have to answer first before buying a dog. Are you expecting a baby soon? Are you about to move to a new place? Do you value having a spotless house? If the answer to all these questions is yes, then getting a dog is not a reasonable idea.

Otherwise, getting a dog should not be a problem. Once you settle all preliminary questions and doubts, the next rational thing to do is to prepare your house.

Don't worry if you do not live in a two-story house or have a garage or a wide backyard for your dog. Since French bulldogs are small, they don't demand too much space. This quality tends to make Frenchies the perfect apartment or condominium dwellers.

They are also likely to prefer staying indoors than outdoors. Given these unique characteristics of the French bulldogs, so long as you have a roof over your head, whatever form your house comes in should not be an issue.

Remember that getting a puppy is a lot like having a new baby. This means that, like a baby, French bulldogs have the tendency to eat whatever they lay their eyes on.

To avoid accidents, you are advised to 'dog-proof' your home. A helpful exercise is to go down on the floor, perhaps kneel, and keep your eye level the same as your dog's. Your view in that particular position is the world from your pet's perspective. Everything that catches your sight most likely catches your dog's too.

To safeguard your dog, make sure the electrical cords and cleaning supplies are kept in their proper places while chocolates and poison (for pests) are properly hidden. Ensure that the floor is free from clutter like small toys.

Your French bulldog should not be allowed to loiter around the house especially if it has not been house trained yet. Before your pup is house training, keep your cleaning tools handy.

Usually, dog owners choose to keep French bulldogs inside the kitchen since mopping the kitchen floors is not much of a hassle. You can effectively contain your French bulldogs inside the kitchen by attaching a doggy gate to the doors. The plastic or pressure-fitted variety of doggy gates will allow your dogs to still see what is on the other side without feeling too detached from the home environment.

The 30-inch doggy gates are usually enough for French bulldogs since they do not grow tall. But if you own a dog that moonlights as an escape artist, you are recommended to get a much taller doggy gate. Containing your dog in a specific area will also help in letting your dog know which specific areas of the house it is allowed to do its business in.

Are French Bulldogs or Their Puppies Aggressive Toward Other People?

It is in the nature of bulldogs to be aggressive. Even French bulldogs, despite their small structure and cuddly appearance, can sometimes be aggressive toward people.

Aggression, of course, is not always the case for the Frenchies. It will be unfair to tag them as undesirable and aggressive. Like humans, each French bulldog is unique.

As a dog owner, you are also largely responsible for the behaviour of your pup toward other people. Even dog breeds that are generally known to be aggressive like the pit bull will not show any hint of aggression toward a stranger if they are not trained by their owner to do so. Hence, the behaviour of a French bulldog is often defined by and speaks volumes of how they were effectively raised and trained by their owners. With proper training, French bulldogs can establish a close relationship with everyone they meet.

Like aggression, dominance is a trait that comes naturally to French bulldogs. As much as they are likely to assert their dominance over the rest of the litter, they also tend to assert their dominance to people. They do this by growling—or, worse, biting—at people who come intimately close to their human.

Needless to say, getting frustrated is not the best way to react once your dog shows the slightest hint of aggression or dominance. Mirroring the behaviour by responding with aggression will not help your furry friend. Fortunately, as a dog owner, there is a lot that you can do to control how your dog reacts to other people. Here are some good practices:

- **Exercise.** While we know that French bulldogs are not exactly a fan of tiresome activities, it does not mean you should not give them exercise. Don't forget the benefits of exercise especially in helping put their aggression at bay. How will exercise help exactly? It will help get rid of your dog's excess energy that it can otherwise use for aggression.

- **Reward good behaviours and downplay bad ones.** Reinforcing positive behaviours and downplaying negative ones is a psychology trick that works for humans and pets. When your furry friends are behaving nicely, you can reinforce the behaviour through toys, food, or valuable attention. Make sure to communicate it to them that their bad behaviour is, well, bad. For example, when your dog suddenly bites your finger while playing, react accordingly by shouting, 'Ouch!' These little yet helpful hints will guide your dog in choosing which behaviour to repeat and which to stop.

- **Show your furry friend who the real boss is.** Don't let the dog be successful in asserting its dominance over you. You can do this not through violence or aggression. You can set yourself as the leader of the pack by setting clear rules and boundaries.

- **Be strict and consistent.** It really is challenging to not give in to every whim and wish of your pet, but remember tolerating its violent behaviour will only give you endless headaches-especially when it grows up!

Are French Bulldogs or Their Puppies Aggressive Toward Other Dogs?

How do French bulldogs fare with other dogs? This one is quite difficult to answer. While some types of breeds are known for a specific set of qualities, each dog is essentially unique. Different dog owners of French bulldogs have varying anecdotes to share when answering this specific question.

Here are a couple of general truths dog owners need to know about French bulldogs in terms of their relationship with other breeds:

- **French bulldogs generally get along with other breeds.** This does not come as a surprise since Frenchies are known to be friendly and easy-going. Given their quiet nature, French bulldogs seldom pick a fight with other dogs especially if they are not provoked or teased. This is also especially true with French bulldogs who are trained well and who easily get along with people.

- **It is no secret that French bulldogs are quite the attention seeker.** They crave for their owner's attention, and that is adorable at times. In some cases, however, they may show this tendency to be territorial with their owner. This means that they may feel threatened, if not jealous, whenever the owner gets friendly with other dogs. Once this happens, a French bulldog will likely pick a fight with the dog it perceives as a rival to the precious attention of its owner.

- **French bulldogs seem to be oblivious of their small size.** According to the experiences shared by many French bulldog owners, when they are placed in a group of dogs, French bulldogs will likely want to assume the position of the leader of the pack. This can be attributed to the stubborn nature of the Frenchies. In some cases, this can cause a problem especially if there are other dogs who may want to lead the pack as well or if other dogs refuse to recognise the Frenchies as the pack leader.

French bulldogs are as stubborn as much as they are friendly. Considering this, there are a couple of suggestions that dog owners are advised to observe when deciding to put a French bulldog with other breeds:

- **Always consider the size of the Frenchies.** It may not be wise to mix small and big dogs together. Otherwise, you run the risk of having your bigger dogs hurt, intentionally or not, smaller dogs like the French bulldogs. If you intend to have more than one breed in your house, consider getting more small dogs to go along with your Frenchie. These include Labradors, Boxers, other kinds of bulldogs, or Greyhounds.
- **Avoid pairing two pups together.** Contrary to popular belief, getting two young dogs is not a wise idea. In this scenario, there are two possibilities: they can fight with each other or result in one getting too stressed when the other pair is absent. If you pair your French bulldog with another pup, the Frenchie will also likely become more assertive, leaving the other submissive. In this situation, the submissive dog will fail to maximise and develop its full dog potential.

- **Don't even consider keeping two same-sex French bulldogs together.** This dominant breed coming in pairs of the same sex, is more often than not a recipe for disaster.

Will French Bulldogs or Their Puppies Be Aggressive Toward Other Animals?

Do French bulldogs get along well with other animals?

Just like the question on whether they will get along with other dogs, this question is difficult to answer.

But if we are to base our answer with the many anecdotes of dog owners that are available online, it is safe to conclude that French bulldogs have generally been good around other pets, especially cats. The key is a proper introduction.

This is especially true among pups. If dog owners start the training while the dogs are still young, French bulldogs will likely grow old being comfortable with the presence of other animals. Training them while young will also solidify their foundation and character as an obedient and loving companion.

Notwithstanding this positive observation, it is safe to assume that not all French bulldogs will easily open up with other animals. After all, the breed is known for its occasional aggressive behaviour. They can also be stubborn. Having this kind of mind-set is helpful for dog owners who want to be fully aware and prepared for all the possible challenges that may arise in dog ownership.

Here are helpful steps to make sure your French bulldog will get along well with the rest of animals in the household:

- **Be patient.** Definitely, trying to introduce two different pets prematurely will not contribute anything positive. It will only result in anxiety and intimidation among your pets. When trying to introduce a new pet to your old one, it is important to take your time. In no time at all, your two pets will turn into the best of buddies.

- **Ease your French bulldog and other pets to the relationship.** Don't force them to get along well. For example, you can first contain them in a playpen for the purpose of introducing the two pets. Observe the response of your French bulldog and your other pet. If neither behaves negatively, then you proceed by introducing them while on leashes. If nothing changes with their positive behaviour, then you can put the two pets together while under close supervision. Just like in any relationship, you have to take small steps in making sure that the relationship among your pets works.

- **Closely observe them.** No matter how positive they have been behaving, it is most recommended to put them under close observation even after their initial interaction.

- **Don't shelter your dog.** Even before deciding to add another pet in the household, make sure your French bulldog is already exposed to other animals. You can do this by visiting your neighbour's cat or frequently walking your dog around the neighbourhood. Doing these simple activities is just like setting the stage for a pet-friendly household. When the time comes that you acquire another pet for the household, your French bulldog will likely be more comfortable with the presence of other animals.

Why Are French Bulldogs Small?

One of the things people love so much about the French bulldogs is that they are small and cuddly.

It's difficult not to take a second look when you see a French bulldog. Its appearance is beyond impressionable. The dog sports a pair of large bat-like ears and a flat nose. Putting the two features together also results in a soulful expression that is hard not to notice.

Do not be fooled by its small size, however. French bulldogs are incredibly solid for their height and weight. Compared to other breeds of the same size, the shoulder height of French bulldogs relative to their bone and muscle weight is impressive. Male Frenchies weigh an average of 30 pounds (14 kilograms) while females around 26 pounds (12 kilograms).

It is small and stocky yet heavy for its small size. The French bulldog sports a broad chest, which narrows down to the hips. Its muzzle is wrinkled and has a top lip, which overhangs the bottom one in a classic pout familiar in every bulldog breed.

Most of all, it has the look of a bulldog but a size of a Chihuahua. Who will not fall in love with that?

One of the defining characteristics of the French bulldogs is their size. Ever wondered why they do not grow beyond 15 inches tall?

The answer to that question is not at all good news.

All French bulldogs suffer from a particular type of dwarfism known as chondrodystrophy. This is also the root cause of the known genetic health problems common in the dog breed like back problems, oversized heads, and narrow hips. In fact, female French bulldogs are not capable of giving birth naturally precisely because of their narrow hips.

Aside from that, French bulldogs also find it difficult to copulate (have sex). This gives rise to artificial insemination among the breed. Due to their not-so-common proportions, male French bulldogs have a hard time reaching the females to fertilise them. This results in the big number of French bulldogs that are produced through artificial insemination.

Pups also need to be delivered via Caesarean section, part of the reason why French bulldogs do not come at cheap prices. While these make French bulldog pups more expensive from other purebred dogs, it makes it easier for breeders to flag potential health threats during the process.

Chondrodystrophy is characterised by a disorder in the formation of the dog's cartilage, the specialised and tough connective tissue that serves as the foundation for bone development. French bulldogs are not the only breed that suffers from this hereditary dwarfism.

Other chondrodystrophic breeds include Corgi, Pug, Dachshund, Lhasa Apso, Poodle, Shih Tzu, Beagle, Basset Hound, and Pekinese.

Other breeds may also suffer from chondrodystrophic. When non-chondrodystrophic breeds suffer from this intervertebral disc disease, they may begin exhibiting symptoms from 8 to 10 years.

Most of the genetic health problems of French bulldogs are rooted in their physical feature. It is impossible to avoid chondrodystrophy and the symptoms it causes when acquiring a Frenchie. When you decide on getting a French bulldog, you have to accept the fact that it will exhibit the features of this type of dwarfism.

Does the French Bulldog Breed Have Any Serious Genetic Health Issues?

It's a given truth: some dogs are more predisposed to certain health problems than the others. Despite their popularity, the French bulldog is actually a high-profile breed when it comes to hereditary health concerns. In layman's terms, French bulldogs can be quite sickly.

If you are gearing to buy a French bulldog as a pet, you should prepare yourself for the possible health problems that your future furry friend may encounter as it grows up. You should be fully aware of these health problems so you can appropriately address them in case they become an issue while raising your dog. Knowing these health problems should not also discourage you from getting a French bulldog. Instead, it should help prepare you to be a responsible dog owner.

In this chapter, we will tackle the different health problems French bulldogs are predisposed to and the many ways dog owners can do to address them.

Reproductive Problems

French bulldogs are pricey for a reason, and one of these is the difficulty of breeding. As a responsible dog owner, you should be fully aware how their size and conformation issues affect the whole process of reproduction from conception to birth.

Due to their size and deep chest, male French bulldogs find it challenging, if not impossible, to reach female Frenchies during copulation. This is the reason why breeders employ artificial insemination to ensure successful conception.

On the other hand, because heads of puppies are normally larger than the hips of French bulldogs, as many as 80 percent of these puppies are delivered through Caesarean section.

Compromised Breathing

French bulldogs have shorter airways because of the structure of their muzzle. This physical trait present in all French bulldogs contributes to their compromised breathing system.

The short muzzles of French bulldogs also contribute to their low tolerance for heat. The shortness of the muzzle may make it difficult for Frenchies to pant effectively, a breathing exercise vital for maintaining body temperature.

Spine Abnormality

Ever wondered why French bulldogs are small compared to their other bulldog cousins? It is because the breed suffers from a particular type of dwarfism known as chondrodysplasia. Some experts attribute the tendency of French bulldogs to develop a misshapen spine to this type of dwarfism.

How pervasive is the spine problem among Frenchies? Studies show that 95 percent of French bulldogs in America are suffering from an abnormal spine. It can also be hereditary. Because of this, ask your breeder if both parents showed spinal problems in X-ray scans before you decide to adopt a Frenchie.

Remember that pets can develop intervertebral disc disease (IVDD) without showing any symptoms. In many cases, however, French bulldogs develop pain in the neck or back between the ages of four and eight. Seeing your dog having difficulty in lifting their head or losing interest in food should be a red flag. When diagnosed during its early stage, your dog may be prescribed anti-inflammatory medications and strict bedrest. In cases where the IVDD has progressed, however, surgery coupled with physical therapy may be required.

What Are the Pros and Cons of Having French Bulldogs or French Bulldog Puppies?

While there is no doubt that French bulldogs are lovable, they are unfortunately not suitable for everyone.

It is not enough to decide on getting a French bulldog based solely on its physical attributes. Before you take the final and irrevocable step of taking home a French bulldog to your home, you should ensure it matches your personality, lifestyle, and schedule.

To guide your decision in choosing a pet, read about the experiences of other dog owners and weigh the advantages and disadvantages of owning a French bulldog. There are a couple of blogs and essays available online that describe what living with a French bulldog is like. Nevertheless, they all agree on one thing: owning a French bulldog is not a walk in the park, but it is definitely worth all the trouble.

Below is a list of pros and cons of owning a French bulldog:

Advantages

- They are affectionate and adorable. French bulldogs provide infinite happiness to any dog owner.
- Their size makes them suitable for apartment and condominium owners. This means that they can be flexible to their environment and would definitely not mind not living in a house with a big backyard.
- They don't bark much. They often only bark when they are seeking for attention or when they want to be cuddled.
- Dog owners agree that French bulldogs are perfect as family dogs. They are small and generally caring.
- They will definitely make you laugh. French bulldogs have earned the reputation for having a light and happy nature. Their wrinkled muzzle makes their smile pretty contagious.

Disadvantages

- The size and body structure of the French bulldogs make them predisposed to a couple of health conditions. These include problems involving their breathing, spine, and legs.
- French bulldogs are stubborn learners. It would take an immense amount of patience and persistence to train them about the basics of living in a house. You have to develop and

maintain a schedule of training, if you are determined to teach it basic house rules.

- French bulldogs do not swim. They will just sink in the pool! They are neither runners. In fact, contrary to what its size may suggest, French bulldogs are not active.

- They can produce bad gas. There is an array of factors that contribute to smelly farts including low-quality diet, lack of exercise, and lactose intolerance.

- If not trained properly, they could respond aggressively to strangers. Do not be fooled by their size. Most of the time, French bulldogs can be territorial especially when they assume that they are the boss in a room.

Finding French Bulldogs for Sale or French Bulldog Puppies for Sale

Photo 11. Want to buy a French bulldog: get one from a reputable seller or breeder (not in a pet store however seemingly convenient!).

The next step after taking all that information from the previous chapters about your prospective baby is to look for a good French bulldog breeder that will give you a healthy pet.

Chapter 4 is dedicated to tips on how to spot on a good French bulldog breeder. This is particularly important when you are purchasing a Frenchie.

We all know that those puppies are expensive at around $1,400 (£1,130), and buying the supplies for them will also cost you a lot. Finding a cheaper deal may not necessarily save you money, especially if you buy from shady dealers, as the dog may have health concerns in the long run.

If you are planning to adopt a French bulldog, this chapter will prove useful as well. This will give you an idea of the adoption process.

How to Find and Recognise Good French Bulldog Breeders

Once you have finally decided you want to bring a Frenchie into your life, it is incredibly easy to get excited about your possible little fellow and jump straight to handing your money over a breeder. Being overwhelmed with emotions may give you the results you don't like. You, therefore, need to be cautious about where you buy your new companion.

In this day and age, it is very easy to pose as a seller on the Internet. All one has to do is to create a profile on a social media platform and extort money from buyers. As a future

French bulldog owner, you need to be very wary of these scams. Below are some tips for finding and recognising a good French bulldog breeder.

Where to Buy a French Bulldog

If your initial thought is to buy a puppy from a breeder, then you must always keep in mind to buy one that is registered with the AKC as any other registry should be considered fake or a scam. (If you have stumbled upon one, make sure to report it!)

You may visit the website of the AKC and find local breeders near your home. Alternatively, you may call them to assist you in finding a local breeder in your state or region. Keep in mind, however, that the good breeders may require you to drive several miles away from home just to pick up your future companion.

What to Look For in French Bulldog Breeders

To avoid headaches, you need to find a good breeder when purchasing your French bulldog. When you think you have found the one, keep the following tips in mind before handing out your money and taking your dog home:

- Good French bulldog breeders make sure their puppies are registered with the AKC as it is the only legitimate DNA- and pedigree-based canine kennel club in America. If you visit a kennel, always ask where they register their litters. AKC requires breeders who sell puppies to register and pay a small fee for each puppy in a litter. If they are legitimate breeders, they will easily fill you in with this information.

- Good breeders have large spaces on their site or home to breed their dogs. Always ask for a tour of their breeding facilities and accommodations for their Frenchies. A good breeder has the right equipment and buildings for their puppies to eat, play, and live. It is a sign that they treat their puppies well.

- Good breeders know what they are doing. Make sure to be prepared to ask questions and openly discuss what they know about their puppies. They should have a complete grasp of the breed: its history, health issues, and nuances. They should be able to talk to you about these without hesitation. Breeding Frenchies is hard, and it takes a lot of effort and dedication for a breeder to produce healthy puppies.

- A good breeder cares about their puppy. They will be as inquisitive as you are. They will ask you why you want a Frenchie, or they will even ask you about the setup at home. Expect or even invite them to visit your home after seeing their breeding quarters. It will give them an idea how you will take care of the dog, and they can even give you tips on setting up the crate.

- Good breeders provide a breeder's warranty. It is essential to guarantee that your puppy will not have health issues or genetic disabilities that the breeder could have prevented by not breeding sick Frenchies.

The Tell-Tale Signs of Bad French Bulldog Breeders

It is easy to spot a bad French bulldog breeder. Some bad breeders are guilty of mistreatment. Some of them do not provide a healthy living environment for the puppies or operate a puppy mill to earn huge money. Buying from bad breeders perpetuates exploitation of dogs and can end up costing you a lot of money in the long run.

Good breeders never treat breeding just as a means to earn a profit. For most responsible breeders, their perspective is to perpetuate the breed and improve the overall well-being of Frenchies.

If you have followed some of the tips mentioned earlier in finding a good breeder, then you will find it easy to tell whether a breeder is a bad one.

Signs That Your Breeder Is a Bad Breeder

1. **If they do not want to meet you at their breeding facility, something is fishy.**

    Always insist to meet your breeder at their breeding facility so you can find out yourself the breeding conditions at their kennel. It gives you insight on whether or not the breeder is a good one.

2. **If you are finally visiting their kennel and you see signs that the French bulldogs are being neglected in their breeding quarters, then you need to inspect more.**

    Check if the facilities are dirty or if the dogs have skin abrasions or sores. If there is lack of sanitation, you may call the police or local animal welfare officials and report what you have seen.

3. **Be cautious of breeders who use puppy sales sites.**

Sure, they may have their own platform on the Internet today as it is easier to transact online, but you need to be wary of those. Some may be engaging in a scam. If they are not on the AKC Breeder Search Tool or in French bulldog sub-club directories, then you may be looking at the wrong place.

4. **Do your own research on your prospective breeder.**

Make sure to look up about them on Google or other search engines before you contact the breeder. A quick search will help you find out whether they were complaints from previous buyers or reports of bad quarter conditions. If you find any, those are easy red flags.

French Bulldog Adoption or French Bulldog Rescue

Despite the upward trend of breeding Frenchies and selling them to their new owners, there are actually a lot of them in adoption shelters, waiting to be taken to a new home.

Many dogs end up in shelters because owner expectations and reality do not meet. That little French bulldog puppy ends up more energetic than they thought it will be or that Frenchie is difficult to train. The list goes on.

If you are thinking of adopting a dog instead of buying a puppy, then you should consider this question: 'Are you ready to adopt a rescue dog?'

This question is important as adopting dogs is not just a cheaper alternative to purchasing puppies. For some, it is actually about saving them, giving them a loving family, and fulfilling their purpose as a companion dog.

Why Should I Adopt a Rescue Dog?

Dogs in adoption shelters only wait for two things: either a new home or death. Oftentimes, many people believe that dogs are there because of some preconceived notions such as something is wrong with them or that maybe they are sick or not purebred. Usually, people believe that dogs are in shelters because they are strays or that they are too uncontrollable police have to get them. These are all myths.

In reality, owners give them up because they can no longer keep up with the financial costs of having a dog or that they are moving to places where dogs are not allowed.

Finding a dog in an animal shelter also gives you the opportunity to look for a companion that will fit your personality. You will be able to learn more about its history as well. Shelters keep records identifying whether the dogs are good with kids or with other dogs or animals, whether they are trained already, or any other health concern you may want to ask.

Adopting Rescue Dogs

If you think you are ready to adopt, then you may check some of these reputable French bulldog rescue organisations: French Bulldog Rescue Network, S.N.O.R.T., French Bulldog Village Rescue, or Chicago French Bulldog Rescue Network.

The requirements are simple but will demand your home and families' readiness. Once you apply, several calls and home visits will be made to assess whether your family is a perfect fit. Expect that a volunteer will come to your home to check whether you have proper facilities for the Frenchie and you do not have anything in your house that can be dangerous for the dog.

The forms and processes may vary a little, but once application is approved, you will have to sign a contract that assures the rescue group you will take care of the dog and that in the event you can't anymore, you will have to return the dog to their care.

French Bulldog Puppy or Adult, Which Should You Choose?

Uh-oh, someone's messing around big time.

nce you have found 'the one', that breeder you know will give you quality puppies or that adoption or rescue group, then this chapter is certainly what you need.

While you are still thinking whether you will get a puppy or an adult dog, Chapter 5 will help you ease into the decision. It's best to consider your lifestyle and preferences to determine what is best for you, in this chapter we'll go through the pros and cons of each, to help you decide.

Should You Bring Home a French Bulldog Puppy or an Adult?

If you believe you are ready to finally bring a French bulldog in your life, then you should be asking another tough question now: 'Should I choose a Frenchie puppy or an adult?'

We all know that French bulldog puppies are irresistible. Those are adorable little beings whose gaze you cannot look away from. As they are young, expect to spend a lot of time with them during their earlier years of life as you need to teach them all the basics.

Adult Frenchies are a delight too. If you bring them home, you will no longer have to think about puppies' early development stages such as teething or potty training. You will also have to skip training them basic obedience activities or housetrain the adult dogs. Once they get a hang of your day-to-day routine, they will be ready to be your constant fellow.

Choosing between a French bulldog puppy or an adult to bring into your life can be challenge. Before making any decision, you may want to ask yourself the following:

1. Do you have the time to raise and train a puppy?

Raising a puppy demands a lot of time and effort from you as it needs constant supervision in its earlier months of life. As a master, you need to make sure that it is out of trouble. You will also have to be the one to train it or to take it to obedience classes to give it a good foundation on how to behave properly.

If you are mostly home or you spend time working at home with some flexibility, then bringing home a puppy may work for you.

2. Is it important for you to raise the dog yourself?

Take note that owning puppies requires you, as the owner, to teach them everything from scratch. You need to help them form positive behaviour toward other people or other dogs or animals. This may not be a problem for the older dogs as their personality has already been established. (But be wary if they have behaviour issues from their previous owner!)

Nonetheless, if it is important for you to raise the dog yourself, you should definitely get a puppy to be able to watch it over as it grows up.

3. Do you have little kids?

This is important. If you have a baby or a toddler in your family, you should reconsider getting a dog. You may want to wait for a few years as curious kiddos tend to accidentally harm the dog (or vice versa). Older (or more responsible and aware) children can help with the chores on raising or training the puppy. If you choose an adult Frenchie, make sure they are tolerant with children.

4. Are you willing to spend more for your dogs?

Purchasing a puppy is often more expensive than buying an adult one. If price is an issue for you, consider adopting. Moreover,

Frenchies may be easy to maintain, but the costs like buying their food or their toiletries, may be high.

These are only some of the questions you may ask yourself or your family before taking that jump in bringing home either a puppy or an adult Frenchie.

Choosing the Right Mini French Bulldog

If you have answered all of the questions above and you have thought it through that you want to bring home a French bulldog puppy, then the next step is to make sure that you get the right puppy that is healthy and suitable for your home. Do not rush into buying or adopting the first puppy you will see!

It is very important to look for a good breeder as they will provide you with the right information you need in taking care of your pup.

When you have finally sorted it out with your breeder, make sure to check the dog's physical appearance. Some Frenchies may be high or low maintenance depending on their physical structure.

If a French bulldog puppy has an inverted or tight tail, that youngster will require more time in cleaning and taking care of it on a daily basis. If you have a flexible time, this may not be a problem for you. But for a busy family, a puppy with a cleaner tail will be of lower maintenance and may be a better fit. The same is true for overdone wrinkles and clean wrinkles, respectively.

What about its coat? If its coat is other than those colours recognised by the standard, then consider it a red flag. Those with 'rare colours', as packaged by their breeders, may have underlying health problems.

How about their faces? You need to check their nasal opening if these are pinched or very tight as this is an indicator of how much air they will have to take in. If it is very tight, then consider providing a facility that is spacious and will allow them to be able to breathe. Note that Frenchies are usual candidates of respiratory distress and heat stroke because of their physical structure.

You may also want to check with your breeder about your pup's personality. Take time to understand the youngster. Ask the breeder if it acts dominant or submissive. Ask them how the puppy interacts with other puppies or with humans. If you have kids, you may have to skip getting the most dominant Frenchie puppy.

Make sure to also ask your breeder about the health of the puppy. Does it come from a good breed? What is the medical history of its parents? From this information, you will have a better idea of its genetic makeup and help you avoid pup health troubles later.

Lastly, be wary of those French bulldog puppies that are priced very low as this may cost you more eventually. These may be low-quality dogs being sold by puppy mills.

If you have checked everything on your list and your prospective pup seems like a good one, then the next step is to bring it home!

Want an Adult French Bulldog? Here's How to Pick One

If you think you would rather have an adult French bulldog than a puppy, then you may consider either purchasing it or adopting one from a rescue group.

As discussed earlier, adult Frenchies most of the time have been housetrained already and have established their personalities. Knowing this information beforehand will save you a great deal of time and money.

While adult Frenchies generally adapt easily to most lifestyles, consider the following before purchasing or adopting:

- **Decide on the gender of the Frenchie.** Some male Frenchies tend to exhibit dominance in the household. If you have male pets already, consider getting a female instead. Socialisation training will also help them bond more quickly.

- **Some adult Frenchies have experienced time away from their former masters.** They need a new home where they will be able to fulfil their purpose of being companion dogs. Make sure you will be able to spend quality time with it in the evening if the Frenchie is alone during work hours as this will strengthen your bond with it.

- **Having established their personalities already, some adult Frenchies do not get along well with other pets in a household, particularly cats.** There may be dominance issues among pets (on top of what was mentioned above). On the plus side, Frenchies are tolerant dogs. With proper training, they may learn to get along with other pets in the house.

- **Despite being trained by former owners, be sure to give time for training and socialization in its early days living with you.** This will teach the dog how to get a hang of your day-to-day routine and the particularities of the household. Some Frenchies may tend to exhibit excessive watchdog tendencies by barking too much, but with proper training, this may be corrected.

If you think you can commit to those mentioned above, then you may proceed to look for a breeder or an adoption home.

The first step is to look for a good breeder or a rescue organisation. To get a list of recommendations, you may want to contact the French Bulldog Club of America (FBDCA) –http://fbdca.org/ A comprehensive list of French bulldog resources is available at the end of the e-book.

When searching for the perfect adult Frenchie, you may want to look for the following traits:

- Its ears must be bat shaped and upright.
- Its face must be square with an undershot jaw and a deep muzzle.
- Its eyes must be dark and must express alertness.
- Its body must be small, muscular, and compact.
- Its coat must be short and smooth. Its fur should be fine and should come in recognised colours according to standards.
- It must have no sign of illnesses. Its nose must be wet, and there should be no dried faeces near its tail.
- It should be amiable and curious.

Once you have found a healthy adult bulldog, ask your breeder or rescue network about the dog's temperament and behaviour. This information should prepare you in dealing with your dog whether it fits you perfectly or if you need to train it more.

Checking Your Frenchie's Tail

Frenchies have naturally short tails that taper toward the end and cover their anus. This feature is an obstacle each time they poo. At times, some owners wipe their poo door to prevent the remaining faecal matter from drying.

When buying a Frenchie, it is important to check if its tail is up to standard. It is a disqualification if its tail is underdeveloped, is reduced to only one or few vertebrae, and does not cover the anus.

According to the standard, lack of vertebra does not form a visible tail at the base and may be an indication of degeneration. In some cases, albeit extremely, tails of those not up to standards are an inch-deep pocket of skin and can give the owner severe problems.

According to standards, Frenchies should have tails. Those without are considered to be a fault in the breed. During shows, they should not be given any award.

On the other hand, tails too short can cause problems as the dog may develop hygiene problems.

Why Do French Bulldogs Have Flat Faces?

I bet you always wonder why Frenchies have flat faces. As it is part of their distinctive features, most people attribute their cuteness to this.

However, having a flat face may not be the cutest thing on earth as it may bring complications in the long run. Frenchies are among those brachycephalic breeds characterised by their short-headedness. These dogs are bred to have short muzzles and noses. As a result, breathing passages are frequently flattened or are too small.

Brachycephalic syndrome is common among French bulldogs because of this feature. It means the dog has (1) a long soft palate that it can already obstruct the nasal passage and make breathing ineffective, (2) an airway tissue that reaches toward the windpipe and obstructs the flow of air (everted laryngeal saccules), and (3) narrow nostrils that tend to move inward when breathing (stenotic nares).

Some Frenchies may even have a narrow windpipe (trachea), collapsed larynx (cartilages that open or close the upper airway), or paralysis of laryngeal cartilages, making it even harder for the dogs to breathe.

Treating Brachycephalic Syndrome

These abnormalities can be serious as they may cause life-threatening obstructions. The dog may cough, gag, or have difficulty breathing. Removal of the excess soft palate may then be necessary. Staphylectomy or soft palate resection can be performed by using a scalpel, scissors, or even laser. The everted laryngeal saccules may also be removed at the same time. On the other hand, correcting stenotic nares will help improve breathing.

Why Are French Bulldogs Small?

French bulldogs originated from crossbreeding English bulldogs with Parisian local ratters. If so, you may probably wonder why they are so small as bulldogs are generally stocky and wide.

In the 1800s, they were bred to look smaller to make them look friendlier. As toy bulldogs became more popular in England, there was a demand of breeding smaller dogs. When the lace industry caught on in Paris, lace makers moved there, bringing their little fellows with them. Eventually, small bulldogs were imported and crossed with the local ratters.

Is My French Bulldog Lazy?

Frenchies are generally active as they are lively and playful, but at times they would rather rest or lie down. Your pet has probably 'owned' its own spot on its favourite couch. This makes some French bulldog owners think that their pets are just generally lazy, but are they?

The answer is no. Given their physical makeup, Frenchies tend to get tired easily and overheated. Despite that, French bulldogs still need to exercise and stay fit. As this is not an easy task, you must find ways to make them active.

To keep French bulldogs up and about, you must train them to get accustomed to increased activity. While they are young, you have to start teaching them an exercise regimen they can make into a habit. Keep in mind, however, that French bulldogs only need moderate exercise as their body temperatures rise easily.

Make sure you take note of that, or else health problems may arise, which may even result in death.

If you take your dog out for a walk, avoid going at a fast pace. Avoid running as well as their body makeup cannot take it. Apart from overheating, Frenchies may suffer difficulty in breathing because of the pressure to take in air. The best time to bring them out for a walk is during night time or when the weather is cooler. Avoid bringing them when the weather is very humid or hot. This way, you help them stay fit and avoid complications.

If you are planning to create an exercise regimen for your dog, make sure it is fun! Stressful activities will make your dog loathe exercising. You may also give it treats so that it feels rewarded and accomplished. For starters, you may want to try creating obstacle courses for your dog to play around with.

Does the French Bulldog Have Any Serious Genetic Health Issues?

French bulldogs are excellent pets but have several health conditions that they are prone to. However, they are still considered to be the healthiest of the bulldog breeds.

What are those health issues? Below are some:

Von Willebrand's Disease (VWD)

VWD is a blood disorder characterised by a deficiency of von Willebrand Factor (vWF), hence the name. This factor is a major component of the formation of platelets. Platelets, on the other hand, are necessary to allow the body to clot. Clotting is essential when the dog is injured to prevent serious bleeding and blood loss that can lead to shock and eventually death.

Brachycephalic Syndrome

This is a medical condition that may cause a future breathing problem for the dog such as obstruction of the air's passageway. This syndrome is characterised by the unique facial structure of the dog, primarily its short muzzle and stenotic nares. This formation, which is also present in other dog breeds like pugs and even in cats, can result in breathing problems, poor tolerance to exercise, and gagging. At the very least, this makes the dog a heavy breather and prone to snoring. Although surgery is an option, especially if the condition threatens the dog's life, it may not be recommended to puppies born with cleft palate. Instead, vets may recommend putting them down during birth.

Eye Health Concerns

Many French bulldogs suffer from a variety of eye diseases. They may suffer from an everted third eyelid, or widely known as the 'Cherry eye.' This condition is where a third eyelid pops out as a reddish mass on your pet's eye. In some cases, it can be rolled back to its correct position. In the most severe cases, it will require surgery. Apart from this, Frenchies are also prone to corneal ulcers, glaucoma, juvenile cataracts, and retinal fold dysplasia. To avoid this, owners must always clean the skin under its eyes and ensure that those are kept dry to avoid infections.

Back and Spinal Problems

Given their physical structure, your dog may suffer from a variety of back and spinal problems. Premature degeneration of the intervertebral discs is a common problem to Frenchies. Abnormal development of the bones may result in various skeletal dispositions. Parts of the back that experiences most stress are prone to rupture or protrude. Because of this, some breeders believe that only those that have been cleared from spinal anomalies should be bred from to avoid producing offspring with the same issue. If possible, check with your veterinarian whether it is possible for your dog to be bred from if it has spinal problems.

Megaesophagus

This condition is a malformation in the oesophagus (American spelling esophagus).

Complications include passive regurgitation as mentioned earlier. It may also lead to aspiration pneumonia if not discovered early on as a compact airway can prevent your dog from breathing normally. In some cases, your dog may not be able to dispel heat and can be deadly. It is important as an owner to be able to check whether your dog exhibits overheating. Protect them from temperatures they cannot take by giving them access to water and shade.

From the onset, make sure to talk to your breeder or the adoption centre where you purchased your Frenchie to have a clear understanding of your dog's health issues. Knowing beforehand will help you plan for the next steps you need to take in taking care of your Frenchie.

CHAPTER 6

Preparing Your Home for a French Bulldog

*Zzzz! *snores* zzz!*

Y ou are finally near to bringing home your puppy! But before that, you should know about the essential things you need to buy for your soon-to-be pet! Taking care of your French bulldog is not a joke. That is why you need to prepare!

This chapter will give you tips on what your dog needs from bowls to crates, from choosing the right food for your bulldog to introducing a new kind of diet to your growing pet, and many others.

The Essential Things for Your French Bulldog

Are you ready to take home your new fellow with you? After learning all the basic information that you need to know about your Frenchie, you must be preparing now for the necessary things you need to buy when your pet comes home.

There are many kinds of supplies available for French bulldogs, and it is easier to buy what you pet dog needs through the Internet. There are more stores that cater to animals now too.

Puppy Essentials

- Food bowl
- Water bowl
- Collar
- Leash
- ID tag
- Bed
- Crate
- Kennel

Consider Buying:

- **Collars or Harnesses.** We already know that Frenchies have difficulty in breathing because of their physical makeup.

With that knowledge in mind, harnesses are a better option for them. Unlike leashes, harnesses can wrap around their torso. Thus, when you take them out for a walk and the puppy tries to pull the harness, it doesn't tighten around the neck and obstruct the pup's airflow. A collar is important as well because you can put the puppy's identification tags on it. Since it is relatively easy to walk a Frenchie because of its limited movement, you may not keep it on harnesses all the time. With that, a collar will be useful. In the United Kingdom, it is mandatory to microchip dogs (via a small pellet under the skin that can be read by a reader- serving to identify the owner and their contact information). US states and other localities vary, so please check with your local authorities as regulations vary depending on jurisdiction.

- **Leashes.** The length of the leash will vary as your pet grows. You may want to invest on those that are strong they don't break whenever the dog pulls or chews on them.

- **Dog Beds.** Whether it's a pillow or a dog bed, puppies should have their own space where they can rest and snuggle up. Dog beds come in different designs to meet the needs of these dogs. If your dogs have back problems, you may want to consult with your vet on what kind of bed is suitable for them.

- **Bowls.** It is important to keep a bowl for your Frenchie, but selecting the right bowl is just as essential. For example, plastic bowls may not be suitable for all dog as some may chew on them. Instead, get them stainless bowls, which are also hygienic. Ceramic bowls are also a good choice but note that they can break. Bowls can be bought almost in any supermarket and come in different designs.

- **Kennels.** When you are finally bringing home your pet, you will need kennels to help in housebreaking. Once your pup is already home, you need to place it inside the kennel where it can observe its new environment for the first time. Crates and kennels play a crucial role in potty training as well. Of course, you need them for travelling. Note, though, the airlines may require a specific kind of kennel. Otherwise, you can choose kennels that are either wired or plastic. The plastic kennel is more ideal for land travel since it's lighter. While wire cages are strong, they may be bulky and big it may be difficult to place seatbelts around them.

- **Toys.** Giving your French bulldog toys will keep it busy, active, and stimulated, which are necessary for its healthy physical and mental development. There are many types of toys for your little fellow. To exercise its jaw, massage the gums, and even clean its teeth, you can give your dog chewable toys made from nylon or rubber. To make the toy even more attractive, buy one that has a flavour! Nevertheless, find toys that are not so easy to break as Frenchies can tear them apart if they are not of the right material. Refrain from buying toys made from latex as they may contain lead. Many experts recommend giving puppies no more than three toys at a time to prevent them from getting bored with their toys quickly.

- **Dog Grooming Equipment.** Your Frenchie may be low maintenance, but it is still important to keep grooming equipment for it. Buy your dog brushes or combs, depending on it coat type. You may also need clippers and scissors, as well as nail trimmers, depending on the dog's size.

- **Preventive Products.** To keep your pet healthy, buy vitamins and supplements, parasite prevention, and dental care products. Ask your veterinarian what kinds of health products your dog needs, especially if it has a special or medical condition.

French Bulldog-Proofing Your House

Having a Frenchie at home is like having a toddler. Anything can go inside its mouth: pennies, shoes, legs of your furniture, and extension cords, among others. French bulldog-proofing your house is important to take care of both your pet and your home.

Put protectors on unused electrical outlets. This will keep your dog from being too curious on plugs or sockets that it may end up being electrocuted. Also, you need to tie up those loose electrical cords or remove them from your dog's reach.

Make sure that the house plants are kept away from your dog. Moreover, cleaning materials, medications, and insecticides should be put inside cupboards that your pet will not be able to access.

Keep These Away from Your Frenchie!

- Electrical cords
- Cleaning supplies and materials
- Chocolate (very important!)
- House plants
- Medications and vitamins
- Insecticides and poisons

- Garbage
- Fertiliser

Usually, when Frenchies are in the process of being housetrained, keeping them in the kitchen is a good option, and you can use a doggy gate to contain them there. Find one that is pressure fitted and made of plastic rather than a wooden slatted type, which can trap a dog if it decides to stick its head out between the slats.

Keeping an exercise pen is also a good choice, and many people have positive results in using it. You may be able to get it from your local pet store or buy it online. Exercise pens resemble fences that are portable. They come in various sizes, so you can find one that fit your dog's needs. Setting them up is easy, and they give your dog a sense of personal space. You can put your pet's food and water in them, along with its bed. For Frenchies, look for exercise pens that are at least three inches in height.

Supervising Your Frenchie

When your pet is still small, make sure to keep an eye on its habits all the time. From there, you will learn its quirks: what it likes to chew on, if it chews on certain kinds of furniture, etc. Observing your Frenchie will give you an idea on how you can bulldog-proof your home.

Choosing the Right Food for Your Pet

It is important that you choose the right diet for your Frenchie to keep it healthy. There is a variety of choices in the market, which is great as some Frenchies may require a special diet.

Frenchies do not have a choice on what you feed them so make sure that you give them quality food. Certainly, the best way is to give them premium brands of dog food. Some dogs may be sensitive to certain types of dog food. Ask your breeder what kind of dog food the pup eats and stick to it to avoid causing your pet's upset stomach.

Buying Premium Food

As expected, premium food is costlier, but for the sake of your dog's nutrition, it should be your choice. This type of dog food contains ingredients that are richer in lean protein than carbohydrates and grains.

Premium food has also other benefits like higher digestibility. It is also needed to maintain a shinier and healthier coat and skin. For a short-coated breed, poor nutrition is apparent since it can cause dry and brittle hair and coat. Give your pup premium food, and it will look beautiful!

In the long run, because your dog is less likely to get sick and live a longer healthier life, you'll find premium dog food more practical or economical.

Reading The Dog Food Label

Make sure to look for the nutritional values on the label. Does it say '100% nutritionally complete'? Take note of the dog food's type as food for puppies and adults are different in terms of nutrition.

Ingredients should be listed in descending order based on their weight. If you want to know what makes up most of your dog's food, just check the nutrition label, particularly the first three or four items on the ingredients list. If you want to feed your dog with the right nutrition, the first ingredient on the list should be meat followed by grains.

Potential Health Problems

If you do not feed your Frenchie well, it may experience some health problems such as the following:

- **Allergies.** Your French bulldog can be prone to allergies, and the common triggers are not necessarily different from those of humans. For one, the soft wet fur of the dog can become instant magnets of dust and pollen. It can also be allergic to the types of food it eats, even its own dog food, although it's more sensitive to soy and corn. One of the practical steps to avoid food allergies is to reduce grain intake. Don't forget to consult a vet, if the problem gets worse.

- **Farting.** Frenchies fart. But if they fart more than they used to, then maybe you should check their diet. It can be a result of a low-quality food mix from commercial dog food. If recommended by the vet, you may opt for a more natural diet rich in fibre.

- **Hypothyroidism.** It is a condition wherein the thyroid glands do not produce enough hormones that can help control metabolism. As a result, this can lead to fast weight gain. To avoid that, your little companion may require a high-protein, low-carb diet.

Choosing the Right Bulldog Puppy Food

Nutrients needed by adults and puppies vary. Feeding your puppy the right food is important since it is still developing its bones and other body systems. This is particularly important up until 18 to 24 months of age.

While the pup is young (around 2 to 8 months), it is best to feed it two to three times a day. It is recommended to soften hard kibble with warm water until your puppy reaches half a year of age to help it digest the food easily.

Since you are probably training your puppy to poo properly, you may want to feed it first in the morning and then again around 4 to 6 p.m. so that when it digests the food completely, you may have a long time to spare in taking it for a poo before you bring it to sleep.

To be sure that it gets the right nutrients, feed your puppy premium food until it is about a year old. After that, your Frenchie will be able to switch to an adult premium food.

When choosing food, avoid those with many preservatives and fillers. Be mindful of the ingredients as well. Never buy food with soybeans or soybean oil as Frenchies have a difficulty in digesting them.

Adding yogurt or cheese can also help in maintaining bone growth and digestive health of your pet. The dog also likes the taste of these types of food.

Supplements, Anyone?

Make sure to talk to your vet first before buying supplements for your pet. Ask about the kinds of vitamins and supplements you need, as well as the ideal quantity to give on a daily basis.

Introducing a New Kind of Food to Your Bulldog's Diet

If you are planning to change your pet's diet, it should not be done overnight to avoid upsetting its stomach. Rather:

Do it gradually.

As different developmental stages require different sets of nutritional requirements, changing your dog's diet is a practice you should be able to master.

You can take portions of the new food and the previous food and mix them together. Plan it out. For example, on the first day, you may want to mix 25 percent of the new one and 75 percent of the new mix. The next day, it can be half for both. You may repeat the same process until you give it 100 percent of the new mix. You can follow the same plan when you are switching from adult food to senior food.

But here is a big but! Do not switch food for the sake of just switching. If your Frenchie has a healthy and shiny coat, it has bright and alert eyes, and it has a good weight because of the food you're giving it, then there is no reason to waste time and switch food.

Feed them on schedule.

When feeding your dog, follow a regular schedule and make sure that you stick to it. As mentioned earlier, puppies should be fed two to three small meals a day. But be mindful as some puppies may think that a mealtime is the centre of their lives!

Feed them right.

It is important that you know whether you are feeding your Frenchie right apart from giving it the right food.

How much food you need to feed your dog is already indicated at the back of the food's label. It may also be recommended by your vet and depend on the dog's overall health and level of physical activity. As an owner, you should know when your dog is already gaining weight. Know that while obese dogs may appear cute, the excessive weight isn't healthy.

Watch out for the picky eaters.

It rarely happens, but some Frenchies are actually picky eaters. It's not that they will starve themselves, but they may eat only when they're hungry. If you offer them food and they do not pick up after fifteen minutes, it means that they are not yet hungry. You have to train them to follow a more suitable or ideal feeding schedule.

CHAPTER 7

Bringing Home
Your French Bulldog

*French bulldogs can be so curious
they can end up looking like this.*

T he most exciting day of your life has finally come! You are now about to bring home your Frenchie after so much ado! We all bet your new pet is as excited as you are too.

Transferring homes is not as easy as it may sound. For French bulldogs, this can be confusing as this means they will have to adjust to a new environment. Moreover, it can be hard for them especially in the early days.

After all, they will be away from their parents and littermates probably forever! In fact, puppies may spend their first few nights crying and missing their previous home.

This chapter will give you tips on how you can help your Frenchie fit into its new home and spend its first night without feeling 'homesick'. Later on in the chapter, you will also learn about housetraining your Frenchie.

Introducing Your French Bulldog to Its New Home

Once you have purchased everything that you need for your new pet, the next step is to ready yourself in introducing it to its new home!

The best time to bring home your French bulldog is when you can some spare time to play with it. If you have a regular job, be sure to bring home your new pet during the weekend. With that, you can give your new dog the attention it needs to be able to adapt to its new surroundings. It is also best to pick it up during the morning so that it can adjust well throughout the day and will not have much difficulty in sleeping when the night comes.

French bulldogs generally adapt easily to their environment. When your pet arrives, let it get a feel of its new home by letting it sniff around. It will make itself feel at home by sniffing every nook and cranny of your home. After it's done sniffing, you can now introduce it to its new bed.

Bringing it to its new bed may be confusing for the pup, so pay attention to its initial reaction and subsequent mood. Ease your new companion to its bed gradually, if necessary, so it doesn't feel overwhelming for the pup.

Once you think it is already settled, choose a name for your dog as soon as possible. Be consistent in using its new name to call its attention. This way, it can recognise not only your voice but also its name and respond to it accordingly.

If you're living with kids, you need to teach them that dogs are not toys. Inform them that while they can play with the new Frenchie, they should avoid activities that can be physically and emotionally stressful for the puppy. Remind them too that French bulldogs require only moderate physical activity to avoid seriously increased body temperature.

Your French Bulldog's First Night

Your pet's first night at home can be a bit agitating for you and your puppy. If you bought your puppy from a breeder, expect that it will be crying on its first few nights away from its mother and littermates.

What to Do before Bedtime

Make sure that you keep its food and water away after six or seven o'clock to prevent it from peeing or pooing when it is time for bed.

Shortly before sleeping, take some time to play with your dog, which can make your pup tired it can fall asleep quickly. Remember not to let it nap a few hours before bedtime as it will keep it awake the entire night.

Also, let it poo on its soiling area, which can be outside your house, and wait for it to finish. When it does the pooing properly, praise it. This will reinforce good practices and will begin the housetraining process.

Where It Should Sleep

On its first night, it is recommended to let your pet sleep in your bedroom to reduce the chances of whining. This will give your pet an assurance that it is not left alone or that is safe even if it is away from its mother or littermates.

Constant contact throughout the night with your dog will help you establish a connection. However, do not let your Frenchie sleep on the bed with you. It can lead to behavioural problems including insisting sleeping on the bed all the time.

If you plan to train it using a crate, you can bring its crate to the bedroom. Otherwise, you can fence the dog near your bed or create your pet's own fort somewhere in the room. Train your pet not to poo or pee on its sleeping area. To minimise this incidence, you can give them just enough space to move around at night.

If you do not want it in your bedroom, you can let it sleep in areas of the house you have proofed already. Make sure to keep an article of your clothing with it so it can familiarise itself with your scent! If you go for bathroom breaks at night, make sure to check on how it's sleeping. This is also a good way to prevent it from feeling out of place and crying.

House Training Your French Bulldog

When your Frenchie is finally settled, you should start training your little fellow so that it gets accustomed to your lifestyle.

It is common knowledge that Frenchies can exhibit stubbornness at times. If you are housetraining them, be patient and give them the right amount of attention they needed to catch on. And oh, do not forget paper towels to catch some poo! This will help you make everything cleaner.

When to Start

The key is to start early! You need to decide whether you want your pet to be paper trained or trained to do its thing outside. Make sure to stick with your feeding schedule as that will help it learn a habit. If you have decided to train it to soil outside your house, make sure you do it regularly!

You know it is about to poo when it runs around as if it is looking for something. Once you see it's becoming restless, try taking it outside or to a paper. This way, it associates the soil and the paper as its place to do its business. Don't forget to do this before bedtime.

When you are training your pet, be sure to give it unlimited access to water at all times. You may think that a pet not trained yet will not know how to handle this, but this thought should not be entertained as it is not the right way to housebreaking.

Frenchies, especially the babies, need water to develop their bodies properly.

Accidents are inevitable. If you spot it urinating inside your house, pick the dog pup and rush it outside the house or to a paper. Remember, it takes consistency on your and the dog's end to train well.

Do not yell at the dog for doing it. It will not understand the reason. After all, urinating and pooing are natural things to do! Dogs are sensitive to human emotions, and if you become angry, it will only hide away from you, afraid you will yell at it again.

As much as possible, avoid using ammonia-based cleaners as they make surfaces smell like dog urine. It only attracts the dog to urinate in the area. What you can use instead are special cleaners designed to eliminate pet odours.

Alternatively, you can use puppy pads, which are helpful in housebreaking your puppy. The pads protect your floors from your pet's urine because of a plastic backing.

If you wish to potty train your pet using paper towels, choose a space that is easily accessible to your pet and is not in a high-traffic area of the house (like doorways). You may put the puppy pad in the area. Otherwise, your pet may do the choosing, and there's a good chance you won't like it.

Frenchies are relatively stubborn dogs but should be reliable by the age of 4 to 5 months. By then, they are capable of finding their way outside. It may be best to install a puppy door so they can leave to do their business at any time.

CHAPTER 8

Caring for French Bulldogs or Your Baby French Bulldog

Frenchies may be stubborn, but they are trainable.

Your new companion is like your toddler. You need to spend time with it and make sure it gets the right nutrition and exercise so that it remains healthy.

Frenchies are toy dogs whose features require them to have moderate exercise to remain fit. For starters, you may take them to a light walk when the temperature outside is cool to avoid overheating, which happens when their body temperatures rise (and they rise quickly!).

This chapter will give you tips on how to care for your Frenchie from keeping it fit to making sure it has good hygiene. This chapter also talks about managing your dog's diet.

Preventive Health Care and Maintenance for Your French Bulldog

There are several hereditary issues that threaten the health of your French bulldog. As a dog owner of a breed that is predisposed to an array of health problems, you should be proactive by taking the necessary steps to prevent them or reduce the risks. After all, preventive health care is a lot better—and, most of the time, cheaper—than cure.

What is an effective preventive health care and maintenance plan for your French bulldog? Here are some couple of suggestions:

- **Do your research.** This is probably the most important thing that you should do if you are keen on not allowing your dog to suffer from any serious health issues. Being knowledgeable of what to prepare is one big step toward actually preparing. This will arm you with the necessary information on what to expect and definitely what to avoid while rearing your French bulldog up. As a brachycephalic dog breed, French bulldogs are predisposed to a number of health concerns that you, as a responsible dog owner, should be aware of and be prepared for.

- **Bring the dog for a check-up regularly.** Even if the dog is not showing any symptoms, you should let your dog visit the veterinarian on a regular basis. He should provide you with a vaccination schedule that is catered to your Frenchie taking into account their age, sex, risk factors and general health.

  Test for internal parasites so that, in case something comes up abnormal in tests, early medical interventions can be done. Most of the time, dogs do not show abnormal signs for pressing early-stage health concerns, but indications of the disease can already be detected through laboratory tests. Especially with the predisposition of French bulldogs to develop intervertebral disc disease, time is of the essence.

- **Avoid strenuous activities and warm weather.** If you want to keep your French bulldog in its best condition, make sure to keep your little Frenchie cool during a warm weather. Avoid very strenuous activities that can also compromise its breathing.

- **Prevent parasites.** Have your dog take a parasite preventive medication that comes either as a topical liquid or as a chewable tablet. This is administered at least once a month. This option does not only help lessen the risk of having your dog suffer from the irritating fleas, it also provides a better alternative to common cures to fleas such as toxic sprays and powder.

- **Prevent the nose from drying.** To keep it from drying, regularly put on Vaseline on the nose of your little Frenchie.

Ultimately, regardless of where you acquired your French bulldog, you have to be prepared for all the possibilities that can arise when rearing your pet. This cannot be emphasised enough: just like any relationship, getting a French bulldog is a commitment as much as it is a responsibility.

Properly Exercising Your French Bulldog

While French bulldogs are not fond of exercise, it does not mean you should not exercise them. French bulldogs are prone to develop spine problems, which can be triggered or worsened by becoming overweight. This is why exercise is still crucial, if not necessary, for French bulldogs.

If you ask French bulldog owners, they will agree that it is normal for Frenchies to just lie around the house all day. Sometimes the only exercise they get is the occasional playtime with their owners.

While they are fond of just laying their bellies on the ground, it does not mean they are lazy. Given their compromised breathing system, French bulldogs tire and overheat easily.

This is normal, but as a pet owner who looks after your dog's welfare, don't let it happen all the time. You should ensure that your furry friend does not go over its ideal weight by making moderate exercise part of its routine.

Can dog owners make French bulldogs exercise? The answer is a resounding yes!

Before you push toward this goal, you have to remember first to refrain from making your little Frenchie exercise during humid and warm days. Also, avoid strenuous activities. That, in itself, is a recipe for disaster. Instead, make sure the weather is nice and inviting when planning to go out on a walk with your furry little friend. If possible, try exercising the dog at night when the air is cooler.

To make sure they develop this healthy habit of exercising, Frenchies should be exposed to exercising while they are still young. With consistency, they will be able to develop this habit. After all, like humans and other animals, French bulldogs are creatures of habit.

When walking with your French bulldog, see to it you don't walk too fast. Take your time and allow the dog to catch up with you and take normal breathing. You should also avoid scheduling the exercise after meals. This is the time when they are the sleepiest and the most sluggish. It will be difficult to convince them to walk.

Make the exercises for French bulldogs fun and engaging! One of the sure ways to do this is to give them treats. If you make their favourite food as a reward when they go out to exercise with you, you make it easier to reinforce the habit. You can also opt to include fun obstacles and routes to the exercise. This way, your French bulldog will be able to associate exercise with fun and enjoyment instead of a belabouring activity it would rather skip.

Conducting the exercise outdoors will also not be an issue. French bulldogs are silent creatures, and they are less likely to bark at your neighbourhood or at strangers. In fact, most of the time, they will bark only if they feel excited.

Frenchies can enjoy outdoor walks and other moderate activities. Once the exercise has become part of their routine, it can even be their favourite activity next to sleeping!

Properly Grooming Your French Bulldog

Once you decide to become a French bulldog owner, it becomes imperative to ask yourself this: what do you need to know about properly grooming your French bulldog?

Grooming the French bulldog is nothing short of simple and straightforward. According to the AKC, the routine grooming for the Frenchie should include ear cleaning, cleaning of the skin folds, nail trimming, and occasional bathing. The whole grooming process will not be so much of a herculean task given the small size and nice coat of the French bulldog.

Due to the unique skull structure of the French bulldog, coupled with its recessed nose, dog owners are advised to pay special attention when bathing the dog. Water should not enter its nose. This is the common issue owners encounter when bathing the dog for the first time.

Since these dogs are less likely to go out often, you can groom Frenchies at four- to eight-week intervals.

Your grooming routine can include the following:

Cleaning the Eye Area

The large folds around the eyes of the French bulldogs require daily or weekly grooming, especially if these flaps are many and deep. When cleaning, see to it you can remove any water residue to avoid moisture to accumulate. Moisture causes the growth of red yeast, which will produce a foul odour. Purchase special or organic facial cleansers or wipes for the regular cleaning of this area.

Cleaning the Ears

One of the defining characteristics of the French bulldogs is their wide 'bat' ears that perk up all day. These ears are actually prone to catching dust and thus need to be cleaned on a weekly basis. A quick wipe with a soft cloth can help you determine if the dirt and grime that have accumulated in the area warrant a thorough cleaning with ear cleanser.

When bathing your furry friend, watch out for unnecessarily getting water down its ear canal to avoid creating a breeding ground for yeast and bacteria that can cause an ear infection.

To clean the small crevices of the outer ear, dog owners are advised to use cotton buds. However, be reminded to take extra care when using cotton buds to avoid pushing wax down farther the ear canal and damaging the ear lining.

Bathing

French bulldogs may need a twice-monthly or a monthly bath. Start by wetting your furry friend thoroughly with the nozzle of the handheld shower, making sure water gets into every wrinkly crevices and folds. Frenchies are sensitive to temperature extremes, so make sure the water is kept lukewarm.

Next, you may lather your dog's coat with baby, horse, or puppy shampoo. All are specially formulated to provide extra moisture. Make sure to go through the pup's wrinkles, covering the top, the neck, all throughout the tip of its tail, the upper back, and the adorable belly. After this, rinse and towel dry.

Brushing the Coat

To take care of its coat and get rid of those loose hairs, dog owners are advised to brush French bulldogs twice a week using a short-bristled brush. You may also opt to use a shredding blade to pull out the pup's dead coat.

Managing Your French Bulldog's Diet

While widely acknowledged, getting a well- balanced diet, both for dogs and for humans, is usually taken for granted in practice. Instead, we have the tendency to eat whatever is available without giving much thought on the nutrition we are getting.

But this kind of practice should not continue when rearing a French bulldog. A well-balanced diet is especially important for the dog breed that usually suffers from different health problems. Without a holistic diet plan for your French bulldog, you run the risk of creating further problems that will affect your pet's spine, cause allergies, and worsen its health.

Your French bulldog's diet is different from that of other breeds. The AKC reminds dog owners that the ideal amount of food is heavily dependent on its size as an adult.

The best way to ensure that your French bulldog is getting all the nutrition it needs is to always consult your veterinarian.

If you just acquired a French bulldog, ask the breeder to bring some of the food that he has been feeding the dog. If you decide to change the food, slowly add new food to the old food until your furry friend fully adjusts to its new food.

While there are no specific guidelines on what to feed to French bulldogs, associations such as the French Bull Dog Club of America recommend specific meals that are ideal for the breed. When preparing your pet's diet, consider making a variety of commercial dry food, raw food, canned food, and homemade meals:

- Commercial dog foods come in various levels of quality. Needless to say, when you opt for the high-quality food (which contains fewer fillers and more nutrients), your French bulldog will likely consume less.

- Raw food can be either purchased commercially or prepared at home. They usually include steak, heart, chicken breast, ground beef, kidney, and, of course, bone. Remember to consult your veterinarian before opting for this diet for your dog.

- Dry food is preferred by many dog owners because it mixes several ingredients like meat, vitamins, grains, and by-products into an easily digestible meal.

- Canned food is in many respects similar to dry food. Compared to dry food, however, the canned counterpart is the costliest because, according to a March 2009 Consumer

Reports study, they are composed of 75 percent water. Don't forget to make sure the number one ingredient is high-quality meat whichever you choose.

On the other hand, avoid feeding French bulldogs wheat products because they are known to make them gassy.

CHAPTER 9

French Bulldog Training for Beginners

'I'm late for my training!'

As a Frenchie master, you want your pet to obey your orders. This also suggests that you have a good relationship with your dog.

Apart from housetraining them to know their role inside the house, you may also teach them basic skills such as sitting, staying put, heeding a whistle, and going to its crate. Knowing this is essential to training your dog for more difficult tasks. This will also help them to be more alert and focused when their owner wants it to do something.

This chapter will give you the basics of training your Frenchie how to sit, stay put, call it with a whistle, and go to its crate.

French Bulldog Training – How to Sit

As an owner, there is often this sense of pride you get when you see your dog follow your orders.

For beginners, there are many skills or tricks you can teach your dog to make its life fun (and bet it will be fun for you as well!). Among these is teaching them how to sit.

In training your dog, you will be using the following signals:

- Sit, which basically is asking your dog 'to put your butt on the floor'
- Free, which means to move or to encourage your dog to move as you transfer to another place

At first, you will have a hard time making your Frenchie obey you given its stubbornness. All you need is some patience and, well, some dog food as this is often the key in training a dog. With perseverance and practice, you'll get there together.

To start, you need to place your dog on your side where you are standing. With a firm tone, order your dog to sit.

As you say sit, hold a treat and slowly make an upward movement in front of the dog's nose. Its attention should be on the treat. Keep the treat near to your bulldog, but make sure it is out of their reach. As you do this, run your hand down your dog's back and gently guide it to sitting position. It also helps to put the treat near the dog's nose. As it looks up at the treat, your Frenchie's backside will automatically go to the floor. When your bulldog's tub hits the floor, say the command, 'Sit!'

Afterward, praise your dog and immediately reward it with the treat. You can also say, 'Good boy!' when you acknowledge it. Treats really do the trick during the first days of training!

As you release your hand from its head, say 'Free!' and move around. This tells your Frenchie that it is now okay to move.

Continue using the command until your bulldog sits even without the treat.

Repeat until your dog recognises the command and sits five or more times consecutively.

French Bulldog Training – Calling Your Bulldog with a Whistle

Whistle is one of the most important tools for training exercises. Almost every dog owner has one. A whistle's sound travels much farther than the human voice and does not show emotion or panic.

The aim of this exercise is to make your dog respond to a call through a whistle. When working with a dog whistle, you can associate this trick with the two main commands that you need your dog to respond to: sit and come.

Here are some of the commands you will be using:

- Sit is useful mainly because it gives you instant control of a situation. The sit command is usually communicated by one long blast on the whistle, although many dog owners also combine this audible signal with a hand signal. In that case, they do it with their hand raised in the air.
- Come is basically gesturing your dog to come near you with a whistle.

If you wish to train your dog to respond to the whistle, start off by teaching your dog to sit using just your voice, as discussed earlier. Once your dog has mastered this, introduce the hand signal. When your pet has cracked this, replace your voice with the whistle but keep the hand signal.

What if it does not obey you? Here are some tips:

1. Take your dog to a space with no distractions.

Dogs are easily distracted. Your pet may not obey you during training because its focus is probably somewhere else. To keep its attention to you, make sure to have some treats or dish prepared to help you motivate your dog.

2. If the dog is not giving its full attention to you, blow your whistle.

Give a one short blast and wait until the dog looks back to you. Always wear your whistle around your neck. This should get its attention or, at the very least, make it alert.

3. Acknowledge your dog.

As soon as it obeys, praise it and give it a reward or treat. Continue the routine until it no longer pays any attention to you and then repeat the exercise.

The dog will eventually learn to come to you when it hears the whistle because it knows that it will be rewarded for doing so every time. You do not have to talk during the exercise, but you can certainly recognise its efforts.

French Bulldog Training - How to Stay

When your dog already knows how to sit and pay attention to whistles, it will be easy to make it stay.

The Power of the Stay Command

Let's face it. Frenchies can be rowdy and playful. They can also panic, be aggressive, and attack other pets, objects, and people. To give you more control over your dog's behaviour, you should learn how to train it to stay. This command, which can be used with other commands like down and sit, tells the dog it is not allowed to move from where it is until you give it permission.

This prevents the dog from becoming more aggressive and gives it times to cool its hot temper as well as relax. This is also good for you too as it can reduce your stress level.

How do you teach the dog how to stay? Here are some of the tips:

1. Have it seated.

You can gently rub its head or back while it is sitting. Ask your dog to lie down then command it to stay while you are standing in front of it. This should establish your authority over the dog.

Place the treat near the dog, but again, don't put it too close. If it is trying to get the reward, try to move it farther. Wait patiently and watch the dog's reaction. If it remains in its position without reaching the treat, praise it, and say, 'Good stay.' You may need to repeat the exercise several times before moving on. The bulldogs will eventually catch on the desired behaviour.

While doing the activity, you should not make any body contact with your dog. Your body language serves as a hint for your pet to break its position. This is because dogs naturally follow what we do even when we move our shoulders. While facing your dog, point your hand in such a way that your palm is outstretched as you retrieve the reward and then say, 'Good stay.'

Instead of giving a treat as soon as the dog hits the floor, hold off for a second. Then in a calm, warm voice, say 'Yes!' and reward it with a treat.

You can also try to take back the reward but continue praising it. The main objective is to teach your dog to follow a command without expecting any reward in return. It should be part of its behaviour to obey you.

Keep your dog in a stay position for at least a minute. Around this time, avoid giving it any kind of treat. When you want it to move and go with you, you can pat the underside of its chin.

Don't forget to give the dog the reward for doing a great job during your exercises.

Your training exercises should mirror real-life situations. Thus, try to incorporate objects such as toys and sounds into your training! What you're trying to teach is that despite the distractions, your dog should still be able to hear and follow your commands.

French Bulldog Training – "Go to Crate"

There will be times when your Frenchie has to be in a crate. Take, for example, when you're travelling.

Airlines will never allow you to board the dog unless you put it in an airline-approved crate.

Although you can carry the dog to a vet's clinic, often, you're required to place it inside a crate for your, the dog's, the other pets', and the staff's protection.

But getting the dog to go inside a crate is another story. Frenchies are stubborn and may likely ignore it. The last thing you want to happen is to spend minutes battling it out with your dog.

Training your dog to go to crate is essential, but to make it easier for you, make sure you have the right crate. Find a crate that:

- Allows your dog to move including finding a good spot to lie down
- Fits your dog when it stands up—it is therefore necessary to measure your dog's height, length, and width and compare these measurements with the crates available

In the market, you'll find a variety of crates with different designs and sizes. In general, they are classified as plastic or wired.

- Wired crates are better when you're still training your dog to go inside crates. The open divided wired walls will allow you to observe the dog and let the dog see you. It is also economical or cheap.

- Plastic crates often have softer sides and are the ones recommended by airlines. These may be more compact, lighter, and easier to carry. However, since these usually don't have a lot of space, new dogs may find them claustrophobic. They are also not ideal to use during humid and hot weathers.

Once you already have the crate, place it in a good spot. It is best to put the crate in a place where you and your family stay most of the day.

Dogs are typically social animals, and they love to feel like they are part of the team. Your Frenchies will less likely to feel scared to get in when they know their new family is just around.

When you're still training how to go to crate, you can place the crate inside your bedroom and let your dog sleep in it. This will also make it easier for you to bring the dog outside when it has to relieve itself (although it's still ideal to have it do its business before its bedtime).

Don't forget to make the crate comfy! You can put a blanket or towel in the crate for the dog to sleep on. For a wired crate, you can use a breathable blanket over the top to make it cosier and help your dog feel secure.

Get your dog ready. Introduce it to the crate. You can talk to it in a happy tone while it's being led into the crate so it will feel comfortable. The best time to train your dog is every mealtime. You can put its food inside or at the back of the crate so that the dog will instinctively come in.

For sure, this is hard in the few days of training, but the dog will eventually get the hang of it. As soon as your dog enjoys its meal while it is inside the crate, slowly close the door. After it is done eating, you may open the door again. This gives it the hint that it has its own place and that after finishing its chores (e.g., eating), it may play again.

CHAPTER 10

Fun Things to Do with Your Baby Frenchie

Frenchies and kids can be the best of friends.

W hen you have successfully trained your dog with your preferred behaviour and some tricks you want it to learn, you may also try other activities that you and your dog will surely enjoy.

Among the all-time favourites of owners is playing hide-and-seek. Others want their Frenchie to look for things they hide. In some instances, they play tug-of-war with their dogs.

These activities are important for your Frenchie as they will help your dog develop its motor and social skills. The more it engages with activities or games, the more it becomes agile, alert, and smart.

It will also learn values such as self-control and awareness. For owners, these are important because these will help them manage their pets in the long run.

This chapter will give you ideas on fun things you can do with your baby Frenchie.

Hide-and-Seek with Your French Bulldog

When you were a child, you had probably played this game with the other kids. Now that you have your own pet dog, you can also play this game with it!

Playing hide-and-seek is a favourite as it helps improve your dog's recall and maintain its alertness. This game can be played with multiple players. Here's how you can teach your dog to play hide-and-seek with you:

- To teach the dog the rules of hide-and-seek, you need to leave your dog in another room and have somebody else hold it.
- Now that your Frenchie is in another room, you can now hide somewhere in your house or yard. As a start, you may want to hide somewhere near your dog where it can easily find you.

When it gets the hang of the game, you can make it more difficult by hiding in areas it is less familiar with.

- The person who holds the Frenchie can shout, 'Where is [insert the name of the person the dog should look for]?' in an excited and giddy voice. This should signal your dog to look for you. Wait until it finds you. Alternatively, the holder of the dog can bring it out to give it clues on the person's hiding place, but do not do this frequently. It may get too lazy to look for you. Make sure the game teases the dog enough that it is motivated to look for you.

- To avoid the dog from getting bored in playing the game, be sure to offer praise once your pet finds you. Give it rewards as well. You may give it treats every time it finds you. This will motivate the dog to look for you and stop it from getting distracted during the search.

Once your dog catches on, switch players. Make it look for another person. Eventually, you may teach it to look for more than two people.

You may play the game outdoors but keep it to a fenced area to avoid the dog from getting lost.

Have fun!

Tug-of-War with Your French Bulldog

Many people think it is risky to play tug-of-war with your dog. That could be true if things go out of control. When played smartly, however, it is actually a good practice to exercise control over your dog when it gets too excited.

Playing tug-of-war with your dog has benefits. The tugging will help strengthen your pet's self-control and will it to respond to you even when it is excited.

Nevertheless, it's always best to play with caution. Here are some ways on how to make the game safe for you and your dog:

To play safely, here are some rules:

1. The dog should release the tug on cue.

Your dog does not understand initially what 'drop' or 'give' means, unless you have trained it to follow such commands.

When you want your dog to stop tugging and release the toy, you first stop pulling but keep your grip on it. While doing this, you take hold of your dog's collar. Wait for a few seconds. Your Frenchie will definitely not play with itself, if you are not tugging anymore. When it gets the signal and lets off the rope, you may then let go of its collar and encourage it to grab the toy again.

You may do that or you may train it to associate a cue to release its grip. You may choose your own like 'release' or 'give'. Eventually, using the same steps you did while training the dog how to sit or to stay put, it will learn that word along with the collar touch. Do not forget touching its collar as this signals the dog to remove its grip on the toy.

While you are teaching this rule, your dog's release will not be as fast definitely. It should be all right. Your dog will learn this as you practice along. Keep in mind, however, that as your dog gets more excited, it will be harder for it to focus its attention on other things you want it to do. With that, you need to adjust your strictness and let it practice more. For sure, it will take a lot of practice before your dog exhibits an instant release of the toy.

2. The dog must grab the toy again.

When it gets too excited, it may expect to play with you nonstop. With this rule, your dog should only grab the toy again on cue. What you can do is to choose a cue or a command you can train with it. To keep it on a moderate mood, the game must not be too tense.

When your dog releases the toy (your first rule!), ask it to sit first as you hide the rope on your back. This should keep it thinking there is no toy. Out of sight, out of mind. Slowly, bring it out again but not too fast as it may trigger its feeling of excitement.

Say your permission command and then offer the toy again. If you let it play, it would take it and understand that it is rewarding. If it breaks a rule by not sitting or by moving around before your cue, immediately say 'Oops!' or 'Too bad!' (or whatever comes to mind) to help it understand that it has just broken a rule.

Keep the word consistent. Hearing the same word when it makes a mistake will lead it to think it has done something wrong. Once you think it has understood the signal, offer the toy again.

As your pet gets better at waiting before grabbing the rope, you can practice it to wait longer before you allow it to take the rope. With this, you teach your dog to be patient.

3. Keep the dog from biting you.

If your dog's teeth come in contact with your skin or your clothes, even if it is an accident, you must end the game immediately. This should help control the dog if it gets too aggressive.

With this rule, your dog will get the signal that it should be careful when playing. Make sure you use the same cue like 'Oops!' or 'Too bad!' so that the dog will get a hang of the term. If it is still aggressive, you may drop the toy, walk away, and ignore the dog. If needed, you may leave the room or go inside your house. This will give the dog the signal that the game has ended because it has done something bad.

Just a tip: If your dog is teething, do not play tug-of-war as these are the times when they are the most aggressive to chew on objects. The dog can potentially hurt you.

Travelling with Your French Bulldog

To make your Frenchie on-the-go, get it used to travelling with you.

As a start, bring it with you on short trips. Take note that bringing it to the vet should not be the only time it gets to ride the car (or any other mode of transportation). This also prevents the dog from thinking a ride always means a visit to the vet.

Also, do not travel with your Frenchie if it has a full stomach. You know what will happen for sure and you will not like it! Before any trip, you may take it to a short walk. This should give it enough time to poo or pee and tire it the dog will feel sleepy and relaxed during the ride. When you are finally off to leave, make sure to secure the pet with a seatbelt! It is also so much safer to put it in a crate.

Don't forget to let the dog wear its tags by attaching them to its collar. Use two tags: one with your home or permanent address and the other stating where you and your dog are going. If you can microchip your Frenchie with the same identifying information (as detailed in Chapter 6), it's a good idea, in case his collar detaches.

For long rides, you may need to stop every four or five hours. Humans, of course, can take much longer, but Frenchies need breaks more than we do.

When you are on a stop, let it eat and drink to keep it hydrated. Make sure you bring water from your home! Changes in water sources can easily upset a Frenchie's stomach. Bring plastic bags just in case your dog does its thing. Nobody wants to see a random poo lying on the streets especially when it is not theirs to even take care of.

If you are flying with your Frenchie (this sure is exciting!), check with your airline for all the necessary documents you need to bring for your dog. This can include health certificates, vaccination cards, crates, and others. If possible, ask your provider if your dog will be able to fly in a cabin with an airline-approved pet carrier bag. This should make things easier for both of you.

Pet carrier bags are available in the market. Many of these look like soft-sided luggage. You should be on a direct nonstop flight during the cooler times of the day. If you are not certain of the temperature, do not bring your Frenchie or you will endanger its life! Make arrangements with your airline, and inform them beforehand of the needs of your dog.

When booking accommodation, make sure where you are staying accepts dogs. Do not leave them unattended! As Frenchies tend to be overprotective and may exhibit watchdog tendencies, they may bark at other people in the hotel or motel where you are staying.

If you are going on an international travel, you may need to check with your vet if your Frenchie can take it. Each country has its own regulations in regard to travelling with pets. Also, other places may be too hot for your dog to take, so be mindful of that as well.

Most importantly- make sure to have fun! This is going to be a wonderful experience for both of you!

Giving Your French Bulldog Toys

When playing with your Frenchie, you can think of many other activities. French bulldogs are social animals, and they like the attention they get from playing with their owners or with other people.

Giving your dog toys is important throughout its life, especially toys that help in chewing. This need is very apparent when the Frenchies are teething as they are more agitated. They want to find a way to reduce the pain and boredom by chewing.

Choosing Safe Toys for Your Frenchie

Frenchies generally have wide mouths. This feature gives the dogs the capacity to fit in large items inside their mouth. This also gives them the idea that they can swallow anything. This is why you need to be careful when buying toys for your pet. Otherwise, they may end up swallowing their small toys and choking afterward.

Know that Nylabone products and rawhides are NOT the best for your pet. If you give these to your Frenchie, make sure the dog's playtime is supervised. Baked pig ears can also be a threat to your pet. These can become soft when chewed, form into a ball, and be easily swallowed by your Frenchie. The hooves can break the teeth as well. Of course, you do not want your Frenchie to get choked.

What you can buy are harder and larger items your dog will not be able to swallow.

You may buy your Frenchie nylon and rubber chew toys as these are available widely. There are also many chicken- or liver-flavoured toys your pet will enjoy chewing.

Also, Frenchies love cuddling. You can buy them stuffed animals. Those with squeakers are also good as they keep the dogs entertained. These are also comforting toys for your Frenchie during its first few days at home. Make sure you keep an eye on your pet when it is playing with its fluffy companion as it may chew off its eyes or ears and choke on them.

For tips, you may ask your breeder about good choices of toys for your Frenchie before bringing it home. Your breeder should know your dog's temperament and be able to recommend what toy will fit it perfectly.

Conclusion

'Whatcha lookin' at?'

The best thing about bringing a French bulldog into your life is that you see how it grows up and develops from being a quirky animal with a friendly and stubborn personality to a well-behaved, loving dog with proper training and a lot of patience.

Once you have brought it home, there's no turning back, but the Frenchie will make sure it's all worth it. It can love you unconditionally and be loyal forever. It will be one of your sweetest companions!

Training a Frenchie and keeping it healthy and clean can be very challenging. For one, this dog is stubborn and prone to serious health issues. But don't worry, all your hard work will pay off.

Good luck! May you have many, many rewarding years with your Frenchie!

More Adorable French Bulldog Images

A Frenchie Santa baby!

'I'm ready for the trip of a lifetime, Mommy.'

Naughty Frenchie, Be Careful!

Frenchie needs some good exercise too—but not too much.

A Frenchie can love you unconditionally.

A walk outdoors can make a Frenchie really happy.

Strong, solid—just look at that.

A Frenchie spreads some holiday cheer.

It's a beautiful day! Take your Frenchie out...

Boo

Thanks For Reading ;)

Printed in Great Britain
by Amazon

HARD UP
STREET

Growing up in King Street, Norwich
1919 - 1947

Mary Agnes Davey

In memory of John.

Larks Press

Published by the
Larks Press
Ordnance Farmhouse, Guist Bottom,
Dereham, Norfolk NR20 5PF
Fax./Tel. 01328 829207

October 1997
Reprinted November 1997·

Printed at the Lanceni Press, Fakenham, Norfolk

British Library Cataloguing-in-Publication Data
A catalogue record for this book is available
from the British Library

Thanks are due to Andrew Cowan for his initial work in recording and transcribing these memories, and for his persistence in getting them accepted for publication.

ISBN 0 948400 57 9

Foreword

Some readers will be familiar with the name of Agnes Davey, or 'the gal Agnes' as she is often known, from her three highly successful cookery books, beginning with *Recipes of a Norfolk Housewife*. The books themselves were born out of the literally hundreds of talks she gave to women's organisations in East Anglia and her many appearances on local radio and television.

When I first met Agnes in 1987 I must confess I had no inkling of her other life as a 'celebrity cook' (the clue was in the marvellous food she laid on whenever I visited her home). I was working at that time for the Norwich Oral History Archive and it was my job to tape-record the life histories of local people. In particular I was looking to compile a spoken history of King Street from the turn of the century to the start of the Second World War, an enterprise begun by Pat Daniel of the Norwich Community Workshop.

In the course of my work I enjoyed the company of many generous and interesting people, and I came away with a small treasure trove of stories and recollections, a true insight into life as it was actually lived by 'ordinary' people in an extraordinary age. It was of course a period of great economic hardship, but equally a time of great family and community feeling. Much of what we now take for granted - indoor toilets and hot running water, washing machines and fridges, television and supermarkets, cars and holidays, and the many benefits of the Welfare State - were not widely available or simply did not exist. But children did feel free to play in the street or wander further afield, doors were rarely locked, and neighbours weren't strangers. Choices were fewer, expectations too, but life was certainly simpler and perhaps contentment more easily found.

There is a famous line at the beginning of L. P. Hartley's novel *The Go-Between:* 'The past is a foreign country: they do things differently there.' Older readers may still hold their passports to this foreign country, but many others will be glad to find such an excellent guide in Agnes Davey. What follows is her own account of her upbringing in King Street between the wars. She is above all a fine storyteller and the picture she paints is a vivid one, full of interesting characters and fascinating detail, and all illuminated by her wonderful generosity of spirit.

Andrew Cowan

Grandfather and Grandmother with their children

Grandmother with some of the family on Yarmouth beach in the 1880s

Exactly like King Edward

My grandmother and grandfather had fourteen children, and then another two that they lost along the way. Grandfather was a drayman at Young's & Crawshay's brewery in Norwich, on King Street. And my grandmother, in her younger days, was a cook. Ten of her children were girls and they also became cooks, as did their daughters after them, including myself. It ran in the family. She died when I was just six months old. She was only about sixty, and she was blind when she died.

I only knew her from photographs, but she was very well described by my brothers and sisters; she was what they called a 'smart little body', not very tall, a very petite sort of woman, and her hair was drawn back in a little bun. Of course, having had all these children, she looked a lot older than she really was, but she was a very kind lady, and her family was everything to her. 'You're all different,' she would tell them, 'but I love you all just the same.' And from what I've been told, they were awfully fond of their mother.

Grandfather's name was John Herring and he came from the country originally. I think he heard there was a job going at Bagshaw's Mill on Mill Lane, just off Magdalen Road, and so he moved to the city. He was a groom to start with and it was his duty every morning to go to Thorpe Station in a pony and trap to get the papers.

My grandparents had a little boy then, and when he was about three they used to get him ready to go with Grandfather to the station. Well, one morning - and that was a dreadful morning - the boy got very wet and he contracted pneumonia. He died, and of course my grandfather was so heartbroken that he simply had to leave. He couldn't stay in the job. So he went to the brewery, and that was when he really turned to the drink. He didn't drink before then.

But in that trade, that was the whole thing. All the men used to drink - they weren't aggressive or anything, never nasty - but they were allowed that drink, and that was that. It was a lot better than paying for it! And they were very big men. I remember all the men who worked at the brewery, and they were all big, tall men. They had to be when you think of those huge barrels they'd be lifting off the dray-carts all day.

1

Grandfather with the dray horse and cart

Grandfather's job was to go all round the county delivering the beer. Every day he went out on his rounds and at every pub he visited they used to say, 'Come on Jack, have a drink.' Well, of course he'd had ten or twelve pints before breakfast, so by the end of the day he'd be well and truly oiled. He'd be out on his own, and when he'd collected all the money he would get on the old dray-cart, put the horses into gear, and fall sound asleep. The horses would then bring him home, perhaps all the way from Diss - no reins or anything - and they'd deliver him to the brewery gates. The watchman would open the gates and wake him up. All the money would be intact, the horses would be put in the stables, and Grandfather would go home. He'd be sobered up by then because of his sleep, and Grandma would be waiting with his supper ready.

My uncles used to tell me that when they were young boys, and Grandfather wasn't home when he should've been, Grandma would say, 'Go to the top of Bracondale and see if he's coming.' So they'd run from Mariner's Lane, along King Street, and up to the top of the

2

hill. They'd put their ears to the road. There was no traffic at all, and if they heard the clip-clop of the horses' hooves they'd know it was him. He'd be the only one around. That was the only way they knew if he was coming or not.

Some nights he wasn't so sober, and then he'd just fall down in the doorway. One time he did that and it was snowing, so Grandma covered him up with blankets and coats so he wouldn't get wet, and she sat up all the night with him. He was a big man, a monstrous man - he weighed 22 stone - and of course Grandma wasn't very big at all. She couldn't lift him. They honoured their husbands in those days!

But I was awfully proud of my grandfather, and when I was nine or ten I can remember he took us to Yarmouth. Young's and Crawshay's used to have an outing every year for their employees, and Grandfather took my mother and me. They used to go by train, and when we came out of the station we found an open Landau - a horse-drawn carriage - and we rode down to the front in it. Grandfather always wore a Homburg hat, and he used to carry a stick with a little bit of silver on the handle. He had a white beard and moustache, and he looked exactly like King Edward. I can see him now, sitting up there in the Landau with this Homburg and stick. Talk about being proud - that was marvellous! A day to remember.

Grandfather was 76 when he died. He never retired. When he came to 65 they let him keep on working with the brewery horses. He was very good with the horses and I used to go down and play in the stables on Saturday afternoons. That was my joy, because we knew all the horses by name. And of course we knew all the brewery people by name, the people who lived in the brewery houses on King Street. We sort of felt we belonged to the brewery through my grandfather.

Grandfather at Yarmouth beach

Grandfather's Beef Dumpling

Ingredients:
¾ lb beef skirts or stewing beef; 1 small onion;
½ lb suet crust pastry; seasoning.

Method:
Roll out suet pastry and place on floured cloth. Cut up beef
finely and chop onion. Season with salt and pepper. Place
meat and onion into crust, sprinkle with a little water and
gather up edges of pastry to form a dumpling. Tie securely
in cloth and place carefully in saucepan of boiling water to
cook for 1½ - 2 hours.

Grandmother's Pork and Onion Patty
(4 - 6 portions)

Ingredients:
4 lean slices belly of pork; 2 oz chopped onions;
seasoning; stock or water;
Pastry: 8 oz plain flour; 2 oz lard; 2 oz margarine;
pinch salt; water to mix.

Method:
Make pastry and line a shallow dish with half. Dice pork,
season and mix with onion. Place in dish, add a little stock.
Cover with remaining pastry. Cook at gas 5, electric 375°F
for half an hour, or until pork is thoroughly cooked.

Hard Up Street

Our house was always known as the Prince's Inn - that's number three, Ship Yard, on King Street. I was born there in 1919 and that's where I lived until I was sixteen. There were six houses in the yard, and they were all brewery houses, for people who worked at the brewery. Opposite was the Music House, where Young's and Crawshay's had their architect's office. Mother used to go there to pay her rent - about five bob a week.

Of course, Mother lived in the country for a long while before then. In her younger days she used to work at Spixworth Hall. Then she got a job at Stradsett Hall and that's where she met her first husband. She was a kitchen maid to begin with, and then she worked her way up to become a cook - like her sisters who were all cooks. Her husband was a gardener there, and they were married in 1902. I don't know what happened, but I suppose times were quite hard and so he said, 'We'll go to Norwich and see if we can better ourselves.' They had my eldest sister with them then, and somehow or other Grandfather manœuvred so they got a brewery house.

Well, Mother had five children altogether - Bessie, Jack, Billy, Sophie and Richard - and one she lost along the way. Then came the floods of 1912. Mother's husband went down to the brewery to see if he could help get the barrels out of the water. He was paddling about in all this wet, and of course he developed consumption - they called it catarrh of the lungs in those days. And that was that - he died. Then Mother lost her baby, two days later. That was Richard and he would have been about one year old. I suppose really that would be through malnutrition. She hadn't enough food to feed them all, and I suppose she neglected herself. Of course, health care wasn't like it is today. But Mother's parents helped her in lots of ways, as much as they could.

So Mother was widowed with four children, and there wasn't the Social Security like there is now. She had to go to the Board of Guardians opposite the Guildhall, where the Advice Arcade now is, and if you were lucky they gave you some money, about five or ten bob a week. They took into account the size of your family, and if they thought you needed it they might give you a blanket, or perhaps help you with clothes.

Once a month they would send someone round to see how you were getting on. These men would come into the house and they would search it from top to bottom, to see if you had any money laid by. The mattresses used to be turned over to see if anything was concealed under there, and if you had anything new they wanted to know where it came from. They would come at any time of the day, and generally they weren't very friendly, but there was one very nice gentleman. He used to come and see my mother when she was first left a widow, and at the end of each session he would ask her to kneel down and they would have a little prayer together. Well, Mother's ambition in life was to have a little nursery garden - she would have loved that - and he always used to pray for her, 'Oh please God, grant that this woman may have her garden...' She never did get it though.

The women would have to go for their money every Monday or Friday to the Guardians' Office. The Guardians themselves would be installed behind a long table at the top of a flight of stairs, and they would literally *fling* the money down at the women, who had to grovel on the floor to pick it up. That's how they would treat them in those days. But that was a hard old time and there was a lot of poverty about, so people just accepted it. They had to.

Then in 1914 my father came along. His name was Robert Cronk, and he was a soldier practically all of his life. He joined the regular army when he was about twelve and for some of the time he was in the Black Watch. He used to lead the mascot (a goat) in Queen Victoria's reign and before the war he was posted to India, where he had his fortune read by an old fakir. 'You'll die when you're forty-five,' this old man told him, 'but before then you'll go home to England and marry a woman with children.' Which is exactly what happened.

He came to Norwich on leave from Ireland, and funnily enough he was brought home by my mother's first husband's brother, Uncle Len. Father hadn't been to Norwich before and when they arrived at Thorpe Station Uncle Len said, 'I'll take you along to my sister-in-law's.' On the way they bought some kippers - I think that was from Joe Aldous's fish shop on King Street - and as they came up the yard Uncle Len said to my mother, 'Hello Edi', we've just now disembarked from the train - can you cook these?' Then he introduced my father.

6

Father in 1917

Well, Mother was living alone with her four children, and I suppose Father felt a bit sorry for her. He could see she was in 'Hard Up Street', and when he went to France after that he just couldn't stop thinking about her. I think he felt it was his duty to provide for her. So when he came home again he asked her to marry him. At first mother said, 'No.' Because she had no wish to get married again. You have to realise that when these women got married they simply had babies. As soon as they got over one, they'd go and have another one, which is why a lot of them died so young; they were absolutely worn out. My mother's cousin had eighteen children and that wasn't so unusual. They must have got fed up. But father asked her to think about it, and he told her, 'You'll be better off if you marry me. I shan't live all that long, and there'll be a pension at the end of it.' Whether or not that spurred Mother on, I don't know. At any rate, he went back to France and the next time he came home he simply said, 'We're going to get married.' Even then my mother hummed and ha'ed about it, but in the end she agreed and they were married in 1917.

The war finished in 1918 and I was born in December of the following year. When Father came home he worked at Boulton and Paul's for a while, and then he helped dig the foundations for Caley's, which became Rowntree's. But mother could tell there was something a bit wrong with him, and eventually they found out that it was 'paralysis of the brain' - delayed shell-shock, really. During the war a landmine had exploded close by him, and he was buried alive. He survived because his tin hat fell over his face and that allowed him to breathe whilst they dug him out. But it affected his nerves and he had to be taken into Drayton Hospital, which was a sort of mental home.

7

Of course, he wasn't the only one up there who was suffering from shell shock, there were a lot of men there. Mother used to carry me from King Street to see him. There were no buses or anything, no trams, and there used to be quite a load of women going up to see their husbands. They'd perhaps get a ride on a coal cart or something. Father, he used to take me round the ward to talk to the other patients. He was ever such an affectionate man, but the other women would ask Mother, 'Oh, however can you trust him?' You see, some of the men were quite vicious, but Mother said, 'Oh, he won't hurt her, she'll be alright.'

Then in 1920 he died, when he was forty-five, and of course Mother got her war-widow's pension. It took quite a long while to arrive and when it did come she got a lump sum, but Mother was so awestruck by having all this money she wrote to the Ministry of Pensions in London and said she was sure she was getting too much. She thought that was her weekly amount! But they wrote back and assured her there'd been no mistake, and of course after that she was a little better off, she had a little better time of it.

Mother with Sophie, Jack, Billy and Bessie

Your Best Friends

Where we lived in Ship Yard there was a breakfast room for the brewery, for the men who worked in the tun room. It was a bit on the wet side because they were washing out barrels and everything, so they used to wear clogs, and every morning you would hear them clomping up our yard when they came for their breakfast. They'd do a couple or three hours work first, and then, about nine o'clock, we would hear them. There was only one room, with a bench, and they'd bring their goods from home - eggs and bacon - and fry it up there. Then they'd have a smoke and off they'd go. They were really nice men. In those days we never knew what fear of strange men was. They would do anything for anybody. And naturally, your neighbours were your best friends.

If you went outside, you left your door unlocked. You could go down to the coast and leave your door open all day, and no one would ever go in, they wouldn't dream of it. And if someone died, a neighbour would come in and lay them out, or if a baby was then about to be born a woman would come round and be midwife. It was the same if someone was ill, your neighbours would take the children home and look after them. I remember in the summer time Mother would sit on the step to do her knitting, or some darning, and the neighbours would bring their knitting too. They'd all gather round and sit there till it got dusk, talking. You could have a lovely evening sitting on the step.

A lot of the old ladies used to go round in men's caps. The husbands would discard a cap and they used to wear them - not all of them, but the elderly ladies did. One old lady in our yard, I only once saw her in a hat and that was for a funeral, otherwise that was always a cloth cap and a sack apron. They used to wear these hessian aprons when they scrubbed the steps. That was part and parcel of the house, I think, mother's apron. But it was a recognised thing that if you had your family coming for their dinner, say, the women would wash and change and put a little coloured apron on. *Always* an apron.

Inside our house we had one very big room downstairs, with an old black iron stove to one side. Everybody used to have their stoves black-leaded - they polished them up and that was their place of cooking. Of course there was always the grate to clear out in the

Grandmother's Norfolk Dumplings

Ingredients:
Allow 1 heaped tablespoon self-raising flour or plain flour and baking powder to each person; a good pinch salt; water to mix.

Method:
Sieve flour and salt into a bowl. Add sufficient water to make a light dough. Turn on to floured surface. Knead together and divide into pieces. Form into round dumplings. Cook in a greased steamer for 20 minutes. An alternative method is to place on top of vegetables or stew and cook for about 25 minutes.

Mother's Seven Cup Pudding
(So-called because 7 cups in all are needed for the total ingredients.)

Ingredients:
1 cup self-raising flour; 1 cup suet; 1 cup brown sugar; 1 cup dried fruit; 1 cup dried breadcrumbs; 1 cup grated apple; 1 cup milk.

Method:
Place all dry ingredients in a bowl. Gradually stir in milk, then pour the mixture into a greased basin. Cover with greaseproof paper or foil. Boil for 2 hours. Serve with sweet white sauce.

morning, and the fireplace, because it was all coal fires. There was a very large cellar under our house, a huge vaulted place, and down in that cellar were all the wine bottles and everything. We used it as a store room and coal house; it had an enormous door and the coalman would just step down there. Some people hadn't the money to buy coal, and so they would buy coke from the gas works for a penny a pail.

A lot of the old mantelpieces were kept very pretty, with tassels round the fringe, and in the middle of our room we had a big table. There was a longish window, with just one pane which opened in the middle, and that was always crammed with geraniums. There was no carpet, perhaps just a piece of lino, and the houses were all lit with gas light. The mantles were ever so fragile and if you put your match too near when you pulled the chain down that just went 'pouf!' That was that - new mantle. Some of the rooms upstairs just had one gas pipe and there was just a bare flame with nothing on it. So we went to bed with a candle.

There were various yards - Ship Yard, Little Ship Yard, Baxter's Court, Rainbow Yard - and each yard had its lavatories. There was a row of five in our yard, and when my brothers and sisters were young they had to share a toilet with our next door neighbours. As luck would have it there were only four of them, so that wasn't so bad, but some of our neighbours had very big families - one woman had eight children and they had to share with somebody too. There was no toilet paper; newspaper was the thing in those days, and it was my job Saturday mornings to cut all the newspaper up into squares and thread the old string through. But one old dear, she never used to bother, and so you'd hear her boys going down and then there'd be a shout of 'Ma! Bring us a bit o' paper!' She used to drown kittens down the toilet as well; every time her cat had kittens they used to be shoved down there and the chain pulled. But some of them didn't go right down, and then you'd hear the *miaow*. That'd be awful!

We were rather fortunate because The Ship public house backed on to our yard and they had a toilet built for the ladies who used to visit the pub, next to what they called the men's watering place, which we could see from our window. Well, I don't know why, but the ladies never did use it, so one day the man who kept the pub

Mother and Toby in the washhouse steam

asked my mother if we'd like the use of it. Well, we thought that was marvellous - a toilet completely on our own! We thought ourselves ever so well off.

Of course, there were bins in the yard, old bins, not like the dustbins of today. There was something like a stable door and you'd just open the top and throw whatever you'd got in your hand into the bin. Then the men would come from the Corporation and they'd shovel it out. They'd take it away on carts. And in the middle of the yard there was a cold water tap, one tap for about six houses. There weren't kitchens then like there are now, and that old tap was running all day long, rinsing the families' washing.

There were two washhouses in the yard, and each family had its own wash day. Ours was Monday. The washhouse was a brick lean-to, and inside there was a bench for the linen baths to stand on, and a copper for heating the water. You filled the copper with clear water from the tap, and anything that would burn went in the copper hole - old boots, shoes, clothes, papers, anything. Once the fire was started the clothes were scrubbed in cold water and then put in the copper to boil up to whiten them. Whites were boiled and pulled out of the copper with a copper-stick. There was no washing powder till later years - it was all soap and soda. Linen was put through a blue rinse. You'd buy a small block of blue tied up in a muslin bag, and that was swished around in the water. The blue whitened your linen. Then the clothes were put through a mangle and hung out to dry. It was hard work, and if you had a big family the wash day would last from about 9 a.m. to 4 p.m. Then you had to clear out the copper fire and generally leave the washhouse ready for the next family. Very hard work.

Something Dickensian

Our bath night was Friday, the old linen bath in front of the fire. It was an oval-shaped bath with two handles and the mothers used to do the scrubbing in it on wash day. Mother would heat the water in the copper in the washhouse, then that was all baled out and brought through and simply poured in the bath. The bath was quite small and as the children got a bit older it was a job to get in - you had to stand up. We had what we called 'up-and-downers' - you washed down as far as possible and up as far as possible. If there was a lot of children then the youngest would go in first. Mother washed you down, and then you all went in and out, in and out, like that. Sometimes I dread to think what the water must've been like for the last one!

If you were very good you could wash in your bedroom with a basin, and if you could afford it you bought yourself a 'bungalow bath'. This was a long zinc bath with a handle at each end so you could drag it in. Well, we got one of those - I don't know where it came from, someone must have given it to us - but you could actually sit in that bath and put your legs right out. Sit down! That was posh! Then Mother invested in a screen, so we'd be in one part of the room, screened off, and as I got out she would shout, 'Don't throw the water away! I'll get in!' And to empty it you simply used to pull it to your door and tip it into the yard - there were two communal drains to take the water away. It wasn't very hygienic, but somehow we never took any harm, and we did manage to keep clean.

When you'd had your bath you would put on a clean nightdress and line up in front of Mother, then she'd come along with the syrup of figs. That was awful, but you'd have to have it. They were firm believers in 'opening' medicines in those days - that was to clean your insides out and keep you regular! We also had senna pods. You'd put then in a cup and pour boiling water over them, and drink the cold water the next morning. That was terrible! I used to gag. That was to 'send you' as well.

Saturday night was nit night. Mother would wash and brush your hair to get the scalp all tingling and then a pomade was rubbed in; it was like Vaseline and used to sting your whole scalp. It would be throbbing, but it did work because I never once had nits. Other children weren't so lucky and there was one girl I used to sit behind at school whose head was full of nits. Sometimes we would lift her collar up and see all the lice and fleas running round her neck.

In the springtime, about March, we'd have sulphur and licorice powder. They'd whack that into you to clean you out from all your winter ills. It was supposed to give you a clear complexion for the rest of the spring and summer. People didn't like to call out the doctor unless they really had to. You had to pay in those days. There was a doctor's practice in Willow Lane and a lot of the poor people used to go there. They joined what was called the Institute which was like a club where you paid so much a week. It would help you pay the doctor's bill. The only time I ever went there was with our neighbour's daughters, just for the company really. They used to say to Mother, 'Can we take Agnes to the Institute with us?' We used to go up to fetch their father's medicine.

The Institute was quite a big building, and that was 'something Dickensian'. You would go in through the big doors and inside there was a very stark room with more doors. You would go to the wicket and say who you were and they gave you a number, then you took your place in the queue with all the other poor patients. You sat on wooden forms and waited for Doctor Flack. It was awful, but I remember he was a good doctor, and so was the one in Surrey Street, who dealt with all the TB cases. There was a lot of TB at that time, and other things you don't hear much of these days, like scarlet fever and diphtheria. Just down King Street in Abbey Lane there used to be a mortuary, and there was also a house where the lady used to wash blankets for the fever hospital. An old wooden ambulance used to come round to this house and deliver all these red blankets.

But we knew a lot about death in those days - it was all about us. There was a lovely family lived just in the corner of Little Ship Yard - the Moyses - and I remember one of their boys was drowned in the river. He was quanting a wherry and I think the pole got stuck in the mud, and he went in and drowned. And as soon as somebody died, anywhere in Norwich, they nailed a plank of black wood on the outside of the window and you knew straight away there was a death in the family. The body used to lie in the house then, in the front room. I remember at the top of Ship Yard there was an Irish lady who had a very big family, and whenever anyone died she would hold a wake for them. The coffin was stood up in a corner and they

14

would drink and dance around it. When we were children we would run miles to see a funeral. If you saw a hearse, you followed it. They were drawn by horses in those days, and if the deceased was well off then the horse would wear feathers, if not, then that would be a black ribbon.

Most people, if they were ill, they would go to Mr Watson the chemist. His shop was on the corner of Rose Lane and King Street, and in the windows he used to have these marvellous glass globes, full of coloured water. All the chemists had them. And if Mr Watson thought it was necessary for you to go to the doctor then you went to the doctor, but if he could treat you he would. Bad cuts he'd treat, boils, anything like that. He used to stitch people's legs when children fell over, he'd do all that. And he was especially good with women's ailments. He'd always help them out with a little mixture. They'd go there, soon as they knew they were on the way for a baby, and he'd be very kind to them. I suppose he charged a few coppers, but he knew how people were situated for money and therefore didn't worry. I remember him as a very stern-looking man, always with a white coat on, and his glasses, and when you went to him you were a little bit frightened. He was a bit awesome really and he spoke very slowly, but he was kind, and he was a marvellous man for doctoring people. I suppose really he was more of a veterinary surgeon - he used to supply all the people on the Cattle Market with horse liniments, sheep drenches, cattle drenches, everything like that. It must have been a goldmine for him really.

Agnes and her brother Billy at Ship Yard

15

'Wab! Wab! Wab!'

Saturdays in King Street used to be a nightmare for me. You'd have all the cattle coming down from the market on their way to Trowse Station. Lots of them went along Ber Street, but if they were near the bottom of the market then they'd bring them down our way. There'd be thirty, forty, fifty of them all coming along, and if you were out on the street you'd run into someone's house - it didn't matter whose house, you just got out of the way. Often they'd run down the yards, and sometimes we'd have whole herds of them mooing about up Ship Yard because of the wide entrance.

Our dog Toby was part sheep-dog and he would snap around their heels to turn them around and get them all going out of the passage again, but one Saturday a bullock ran straight into our washhouse and got wedged in the door. Of course, no one could get round it. One of our neighbours - he wasn't very big - came out and he tried pulling on its tail, with his foot on its backside. But that was no good at all, so we had to wait for one of the drovers to turn up. They managed in the end - the drover just kept wedging and wedging until eventually he got through and pushed it out.

Some of the drovers weren't so patient and they used to *whop* the poor old things. They could be very cruel, but that was life at the time and they didn't know any different. My brother often used to go bullock-whopping, a lot of the boys did. They would bullock-whop all day, and perhaps get a penny or two at the end of it. They also used to go up to the Cattle Market and come home with bottles of milk for my mother - they used to take a bottle with them and milk the cows in the pens. They would get severely wrong if they were found doing it, but I suppose they thought Mother was hard up and could do with an extra pint of milk.

I don't know why, but people never seemed to cook anything on a Saturday. They would just have something makeshift, rolls or cheese or something. And of course, that was a real time for drinking as well. There was one house in Abbey Lane where the lady would go out in the morning and come home very much the worse for drink, and then she and her husband would have a terrific row. The husband used to run out of the house, and all of a sudden the window would fly open and all this crockery would come flying out after him! Also on Saturdays we would have the streetsellers come round. There'd be Mr Shorten, who came up on a horse-and-trap from out Stoke way. He used to bring country butter, and perhaps a few greens. Our milkman, of course, used to deliver his milk in a can. The women would take a jug to the door and you'd hear his can bang down on their step, then you'd hear him flip back the lid and ladle it out. Then on Sunday morning it was the fishmonger - he used to carry a basket of shrimps on his head and would sell shrimps and winkles for Sunday night tea.

In the summer there was a little Italian man who used to come down from Ber Street in a white coat and straw hat, selling ice cream from a barrow. And there was also a pop man. He had a pony and cart - a small cart with a roof over it; that looked like a little house on wheels really - that would be full of bottles of ginger beer and sarsparilla and what have you. The children used to undo the bottles so all the gas would come out. One man I was frightened of - I don't know why - was called Prompo, and he used to come round selling linen props, shouting his name, 'Prompo! Prompo! Prompo!' The watercress man, his shout was 'Wab! Wab! Wab!' - which wasn't a bit like 'watercress'. But you used to buy it in those days, and you never thought about whether or not that was washed well, or if the water was polluted.

On Good Friday the boys used to come round selling hot cross buns, and the barrows they used would be for gathering horse manure during the week. They'd have a little bit of cloth put in the bottom and then the hot cross buns would be on top of that. You'd lie in bed, and at about 7 o'clock you would hear these boys coming in the distance. They would call out, 'Hot cross buns... hot cross buns... hot cross buns...' and gradually that would get louder and louder, and if it stopped then you knew somebody was buying some. My mother would never buy any because she always made her own buns, and I think she objected to these barrows. But I don't think people ever took any harm from it.

Of course, there was still a lot of poverty and homelessness in those days, and we often used to have the tramps come round, especially after the First World War. They would be men who were injured, legless or armless. If they had both legs missing they would sit on little boxes and wheel themselves around - no wheelchairs then.

17

And if only one leg was gone then they'd be on crutches. They used to play musical instruments, and sometimes a whole band would come round, four or five ex-servicemen all missing a limb or two, simply for the sake of getting a copper. That was dreadful really, but they had to beg because they couldn't get the jobs. The tramps who came would have a billy can, or an old cocoa tin with a piece of string at the top, and they'd say, 'Can we have some tea? Will you make us some tea, Ma'am?' Perhaps there'd be some tea in the bottom of their tin, or cocoa or something, and you'd boil up some water and give it to them.

There was one who came to us who used to play the accordion, or sometimes the violin. He'd come and stand on the step in our yard, with his crutch and his one good leg, and he'd play us a tune. But I'm afraid he wasn't very good at it. So one day when he came round my brother Billy went upstairs and found his own accordion, and he took up the tune - and when the old soldier heard Billy playing he stopped. Mother wasn't at all pleased. She went out and she gave the poor man a penny, and she said, 'I'm ever so sorry, that's my boy doing that.' 'Well,' the man said, 'you can tell him he play a lot better than I do, Ma'am!' But they were never turned away, never. In our house we always had shortcakes - they were perpetual, my mother was always making shortcakes - and she'd perhaps give them a couple of those. Or else they'd get a piece of bread or something. That's if the people they went to could afford it, because some of the people were as poor as the tramps. Many poor children in King Street would go hungry at that time.

Norfolk Shortcake

Ingredients:

8 oz self-raising flour or plain flour with 1 teaspoon baking powder; 2 oz lard; 2 oz margarine; 4 oz currants or sultanas; 4 oz sugar granulated; 3 tablespoons of water; pinch of salt.

Method:

Well grease and flour a baking sheet. Sieve together flour, salt and baking powder if used. Add sugar and fruit and mix with water to form a dough. Turn on to a floured surface. Roll out to ½ inch thickness. Score diagaonal lines across pastry with the back of a knife. Cut into squares, brush with milk. Place on to tin and bake for 15 minutes at gas 5, electric 375°

'Sweets, Pickles and Tinctures.'

There was never very much money in our family, but what we did have we managed to live on quite well. Mother used to make something out of nothing - she'd make a stew out of any old meat bone. They used to fill the children up with dumplings, and I remember we used to have what they called 'kettle broth'. You'd get a basin and cut a thick slice of bread, pour boiling water over that, add a piece of margarine, salt and pepper, and that was your broth. That was very filling, and there was many a man ate that for his supper.

During the week we often had a kipper for tea, or a herring bloater. October was the season for herring and they used to have what they called 'old high dried', which cost about a penny. This was a red herring which was salted and dried until it shrivelled up to a sort of copper colour. Then if your mother had a gridiron, she would cook fish on that. This was a piece of iron with bars across, more like a grill, and it had a round handle. You'd make a very bright fire - you mustn't have it flaming or smokey - and when it got bright and red you'd lay the old gridiron on and lay the fish on top of that. The 'old high dried' was ever so salty and the father generally got that, not many children. The kids would have a piece of kipper - not a whole one, a piece, and when we had a crab, the children just used to get the claws.

We used to have scraps too, which we bought from the pork butcher. In those days there would be butchers and there would be pork butchers. We used to go to Yeoman's or Goodson's, two pork butchers exactly opposite each other on Ber Street. They never wasted anything on a pig in those days. The shops used to roast joints of pork and collect all the fat that came off. The butcher would cut this fat into squares, and that would be baked and baked to make dripping, and then, in the tin, would be left all these bits of dried fat which would be sold as scraps. You'd buy a penn'th or two of these scraps, and dip them in salt, with a bit of bread and a cup of tea. I used to like mine with brown sugar, which would take the fatty taste off. For beef we would go to Daniel's in King Street, at the bottom of Horn's Lane. Amy and Mr Daniel were very nice people and when their son Ernest had a birthday they used to give parties for all their

Grandfather's Tripe and Onions

Ingredients:
2 lb tripe; 8 oz onions; ¾ pint of milk; 1 level teaspoon salt; 1 tablespoon plain flour; ½ oz butter; pepper.

Method:
Wash tripe well, cut into 2" squares. Peel and slice onions thinly. Put in saucepan with tripe. Add milk and salt. Bring to boil and lower heat. Cover pan with lid and simmer very gently for 35 - 40 minutes until tripe is tender. Mix flour to a smooth paste with a little cold water. Add to tripe and onions. Stir until mixture boils and thickens. Add butter, season with pepper and stir. It is then ready for serving.

Mrs Swoish's Norfolk Bread Pudding

Ingredients:
½ lb bread scraps (crusts as well); ¼ lb of suet; 2 oz soft brown sugar; ¼ lb currants; nutmeg and spice.

Method:
Soak bread in water until soft. Squeeze out until quite dry. Place in bowl and beat with a fork. Add all dry ingredients and mix well. Grease a pie dish well with margarine. Press mixture into dish. Dot over with pieces of margarine or butter. Cook for 1 hour at gas 5, electric 375° F.

customers' children. We would buy our beef dripping from them and I used to have that for tea. It was very very hard and mother used to cut me a chunk to eat with a slice of bread. You couldn't spread it.

You didn't have very big ovens in those days, so if you had to cook a large dinner you would take it to the baker's. Our baker was Mr Haydon, who used to be where Bennett's now is. He made lovely bread, and on Sundays he used to cook people's dinners in his oven. It would cost about a penny, and he did the same on Christmas Day. We wouldn't have turkey in those days, nothing like that; the majority of people kept tame rabbits. You'd see all the mothers going up the road with their tins, full of water and onions, and they would be ready for about two o'clock. And in the autumn they used to take big stone jars of apples - windfalls - which he would bake overnight. They used to come out lovely.

For our vegetables we went to Mrs Swoish. She was a widow lady and she kept a general store just beyond Little Ship Yard. There was a couple of steps led up to this shop and then a very small square of concrete that you walked into, and the counter ran right the way round. On one side of the counter she sold vegetables and fruit, and on the other side it was sweets, pickles and tinctures. She used to have these big jars of piccalilli, pickled onions, pickled cabbage, and then her bottles of tincture of senna, rhubarb and figs. Next to them was a plate, and on this plate was laid a spoon which she used to dig into all the jars, never washed from one week to the next. People would go in there with a basin to buy their penn'th of red cabbage and this spoon would be green! We never bought any because we weren't a pickle family, but we did buy our sweets from there and they used to be absolutely fly-blown. With the horses and cattle and the rest, you'd get flies all summer long and they'd settle on these sweets. They were totally covered in fly dirt. And the windows of the shop, you couldn't see through them for dust!

I remember she used to have an enormous amount of potatoes, because she did quite a good trade in them. She lived all on her own at the back of this shop, and when her potatoes came in she'd have the man tip them over her counter. The space between the counter and her living space wasn't very wide either, and there'd be five or six sacks all piled in there. You'd go in and you'd say, 'Could I have a cabbage please?' So she'd go to one side and get you a cabbage.

Then you'd ask her for something else, perhaps some sweets, and she would go to the other side, and all the time she would be walking on these sacks. All of a sudden she would appear ever so tall, and then she'd go down ever so tiny, because she was clambering over these sacks! And once a sack was empty it would stay there, along with all the soil. It would be left there for years.

If you had any stomach upset, Mrs Swoish would give you a tincture - perhaps some syrup of figs. She had a measuring glass there, and that was never, ever washed. She'd measure out the medicine, pour it out, and that old glass would go back on the shelf. And that was that, that was the finish. She never washed it. But my mother used to say she had the finest soft fruit in Norwich - her strawberries used to be absolutely perfect. She always bought the best. And sometimes we'd have a penn'th of redcurrants for our tea. We'd have them with bread and butter and dip them in sugar.

A little bit further along King Street from us, at the ABC Wharf, was the old liquor stores for the brewery - what used to be Whitbread's bottling stores - and then there was a little shop called Green's. Now Mrs Green used to sell vinegar and pork dripping, and that's all she would sell. You used to open the door and go down one little step, and that used to *smell* of vinegar and dripping. And the counter was scrubbed and scrubbed and scrubbed until it was absolutely white. You could have eaten off the floor, she was so clean and tidy. Then on the other side of the street there was a shop called Butcher's. You went up another step, walked down a passage-way, turned left, and you'd be in this little shop. Now this lady made toffee apples and at the back of her shop she sold paraffin. She would be serving someone with perhaps half a gallon of paraffin, and then without washing her hands she'd come and serve you with a toffee apple, or she'd go and get the sweets out. So you always had a paraffin taste!

Next door to her there was a boot and shoe repairer called Mr Cooper. He was a very nice man, but everything in his shop appertained to religion, and his window was covered with biblical texts, like *'Prepare to meet thy God!'* Then next door to Mr Cooper there was a little old house where the boys used to go to have their bicycles repaired, and then there was the seed shop owned by a man called Tommy Reed who had just one hand. I could never make out

22

why he always had a leather glove on, but as I got older of course I knew what it was - I think he lost his hand during the war. It used to shine, that leather glove, and I wondered however he cleaned it. He sold seed to people who kept pigeons and rabbits, and he also had great big dog biscuits. Every Monday afternoon my mother would walk to the General Post Office, where Anglia TV now is, to collect her pension, and she always used to take our old dog with her. Well, when she got as far as Peter Parmentergate church she would put a penny in Toby's mouth and he would run all the way to this seed shop, put his paws on the counter and drop the penny, and the man gave him a biscuit. That was his treat. I used to love going in there to run my hands through those sacks of corn, and there also used to be a little bit of betting done on the side; the men used to take their betting slips in there.

I remember the top of Abbey Lane was where Aldous started his ice cream business. They had a little house in there and they sold lovely yellow ice cream from a barrow. The ice cream was in a milk can, sunk in ice. Then on the bottom right hand side of Horn's Lane there were the coal people, the Smiths. They were two sisters and their father, and these women used to carry half a hundredweight of coal on their hips. They used to sort of lodge it on their hip. They looked so thin, but they must have been mighty strong, terribly strong. And opposite their coal yard was Pope's, the hay merchant. People would go there for hay bons, which was hay twisted so that it looked like a curled up snake. That cost about a penny and was for rabbits and chickens and all that sort of thing. I think they used to do quite a good trade there.

Next to Pope's was Mr Websdale the grocer, who stood in the local elections. He used to have sacks of brown sugar standing outside and my mother used to tell me, 'Don't you get brown sugar from there, it's full of lumps!' The dogs used to cock their legs up on the sacks, you see! I don't suppose Mr Websdale knew. But it was a lovely shop, quite big, and they used to have all these tins of tea - Darjeeling, Ceylon, and all the rest, in lovely big red tins, about three foot tall. Then they had dried fruit which they kept in drawers under the counter. You'd ask for a pound of currants and they'd pull out the old drawer, dig in, weigh the pound of currants and then take out a blue bag. They'd make a hollow in this bag with their hands and pour in the currants, then do it up. I used to watch this and think, 'Oh, I'd like to be a shop assistant,' because I thought that was so marvellous. They used to sell practically everything, and next door he had a little off-licence where the old men would congregate. There again there used to be a lot of betting done, and at lunchtimes the old ladies with their hessian aprons and men's caps would go in for their drink of beer, or perhaps they would go to the pub and sit in the old snug.

A lot of the shops wouldn't give out farthings as change, they used to give you a packet of pins instead. And one of the ways we used to save money was to go in a draw. Price's drapery shop on Magdalen Street used to run a draw, and so did Loose's the china shop. Each person in the draw was given a number and you'd pay so much a week. If there were twenty people and they each paid a shilling, then after so many weeks you would get a ticket for a pound's worth of goods. And if your number was four then you got your ticket after four weeks, but you carried on paying your shillings. They'd have a draw lady in each neighbourhood who collected the money, and I can remember, when I was about five or six, having to take the money to Mrs Smith who lived in Sherbourne Place, nearly opposite the chapel. I'd go and knock on her door and when I gave her the money she'd write the amount down and give me a sweet, and then, after so much time, I'd go again and she'd say, 'Oh, your mum has got a draw ticket this week.' Then we'd go down to Loose's and lumme, for a pound you'd buy nearly half a home in those days!

Agnes with her first doll's pram wearing a necklace from the Wembley exhibition 1926

A Day to be Happy

There was a lot of life in King Street in my younger days, but there wasn't the traffic there is now, so we could play on the roads. I went to Horn's Lane School and usually we finished at half past four, then you'd run home, change your shoes, change your clothes, and play for a while. One game we used to play was 'arrows' - someone would run in front and chalk arrows on the path and you would follow them. We played marbles of course, and sometimes we would go to a vegetable shop and ask for a bit of orange rope. The oranges used to come in slatted boxes and there'd be this orange rope around them. You'd knot that together and the first lamp-post you found, one of the boys - or a girl if she was able - would shin up the post and wrap the rope over the bar. Then you'd sit on the rope and swing round the lamp-post. That used to cut your backside to pieces.

I often used to play with a boy called Colin Nicholls, whose father was the brewery's head accountant. They had such a nice house, just before Mariner's Lane, and I remember he had a tortoise. We used to have races with one tortoise, though how we managed that I don't know. Holiday time we would all go down to Trowse Common. That was our treat. We'd get up in the morning and the girls and boys would say, 'We're going down to Trowse, are y' coming?' You'd say yes, and your mother would pack you up a sandwich or two, with some stale shortcakes, and then you'd go and get a ha'penn'th of lemonade powder, or a piece of licorice which you'd put in a bottle and fill up with water.

We'd be down there till about five o'clock at night. We never came to any harm. My mother always warned me that I wasn't to go near where the river was, but the boys used to go swimming in the nude. We'd sit in the grass and play games, rolling-about games, or pick flowers - buttercups and daisies - and make daisy chains. If you were lucky and you had a ha'penny to spend, there was a shop opposite the common, so you could get a ha'penn'th of sweets or something. And on Trowse Church there was a clock, so we always knew what the time was, and when we should start walking home. That was our day out, and then perhaps we'd go the next day as well. The children from the other end of King Street would go up to Mousehold, because we kept to our own areas. They never played at

Sophie's Date and Oat Slab Cake

Ingredients:
Date mixture: ¼ lb dates; 2 dessertspoons demerara sugar;
2 dessertspoons water. Cake mixture: 4 oz oats;
2 oz self-raising flour; 2½ oz demerara sugar;
3 oz margarine; 1 oz chopped walnuts.

Method:
Gently heat together dates, demarara sugar and water in
saucepan until soft. Rub margarine into dry ingredients
except the chopped walnuts. Line a flat greased tin with
half of the cake mixture. Cover with date mixture. Sprinkle
with walnuts. Spread over the remaining cake mixture and
press down well. Bake at gas 4, electric 350° F
for 25 minutes.

Mother's Coquelles
(Traditionally eaten on Ash Wednesday)

Ingredients:
1½ lb plain flour; 1 oz fresh yeast; 1 oz currants;
¼ oz margarine; 1 egg; ½ pint milk; ½ teaspoon spice;
pinch salt; 2 oz sugar.

Method:
Sieve dry ingredients into a bowl. Melt margarine over low
heat. Add milk and heat until tepid. Cream yeast and sugar
together until dissolved. Add egg, milk, yeast and currants
to dry ingredients. Knead well. Leave to rise for
approximately one hour. Turn on to floured board and form
into squares. Place fairly close together on greased baking
sheets. Leave to rise for 20 minutes. Bake in heated oven,
gas 7, electric 425° F for 20 minutes.

Agnes, aged 8 years, and her mother.

our end of the street and we didn't play in theirs.

In between times there were visits to the cemetery, when Mother would say, 'Come on, we're going up the cemetery.' And that was some-thing because we went on a tram. She went to clean a man's grave and would get five shillings every three months from London. The man had been a Londoner who died in Norwich and was buried there, and my mother used to clean the headstone. She'd have a bucket and a scrub-brush and a cloth which we took on the tram, and as soon as we got there she'd take her coat off and hang it on a tree or lay it on a bush, and then she'd fill this bucket with water and clean the stone. We used to go every month, and she would write to this lady in London to say it was done.

Other times I would come home from school and Mother would say, 'Right, eat your tea, we're going to the pictures.' She was an ardent picture fan, and she especially liked the cowboys. They used to have serials in those days and she would cart me off to the pictures two or three times a week. Her dream was to be in cowboy country. 'Oh,' she'd say. 'I'd love to get in that cookhouse and cook for those cowboys!' I think she thought it was the real thing.

We used to go to the Regent or the Electric on Prince of Wales Road, and if we were flush it'd be the Haymarket on Hay Hill. You really thought you were well off if you went to the Haymarket. It had a lovely foyer, and inside all the walls were painted to look like gardens. They had a man who used to come up out of the floor playing an organ, but my favourite was the Regent. The stairs used to go up the middle as you came in and underneath them was a goldfish pond. It was all tiled and marbled, with a sort of iron balustrade in front, and there was a pair of nymphs, one on each side, holding shells which the water ran out of. I think that was the attraction for a lot of people going there.

One thing which is really vivid in my memory is when a film called *The Sea Beast* came to Norwich. I came out of school one day and there were *crowds* of people in King Street, all jostling around this cart. It was an enormous cart with a huge cage on the back, and in the cage there was a man dressed up as the sea beast. They were advertising the film around the city, and that cart could hardly get through the street, there were so many people crowding it. This was something really out of the ordinary, and I was terrified.

Of course, we had no television in those days, but when we got a wireless we used to spend the evenings indoors listening. My Uncle Ernie who lived in Baxter's Court had a crystal set. It was on a stand with a horn attached to it, and one Christmas there were eighteen of us all gathered around this small horn. They were relaying a panto-mime from one of the theatres in London - *Dick Whittington* I think that was - and all we could hear was this mumbling. Nothing else. But it was a wonderful evening out! .

One very exciting time for us was voting day for the Council. We would have a holiday from school and us boys and girls used to go through the streets singing a little song. I remember one year the Jewson family put up against Mr Websdale the grocer, and the song was:

> *Vote, vote, vote for Mr Websdale,*
> *Chuck old Jewson in the bin,*
> *For she ain't no bloomin' good,*
> *And she's like a block of wood,*
> *And we won't go voting any more!'*

That was Miss Jewson, a maiden lady, and quite a tartar. I think at one time she was Lord Mayor. But really it was a day to be happy - lots of excitement. And another exciting time was Valentine's Day. You were supposed to have your tea without a light on that day, and you'd rush home from school all excited because you knew you were going to get something. Your parents would wait until it was dark and then they'd make some excuse to go out - my mother would say, 'Oh, I must go to the shop!' Or my brothers would say it, because they were too old by then to have Valentines. You wouldn't think anything about it, and then the next thing you knew there'd be a bang on the door. Mother would say, 'Oh, I wonder who that is,' and of course you'd go and look and there'd be a little gift on the step. It wouldn't be very much, a packet of chewing gum or something, a very little tiny thing. But I do remember one year - mother must have been flush or something - and I was given a red cardigan. That was the best Valentine's present I ever had.

They always used to say, 'If you're not a good girl, Father Valentine won't come.' Well, he was a mystery to me, because I'm sure I never did see him. The naughty boys, and some of the naughty girls, used to fill boxes with horse droppings and stick them on the steps. Or you'd get a shoebox and put a whole length of string on it, and put that on the door and run away and hide, and when the poor woman came to the door you'd pull the string away right fast. They nearly fainted sometimes! But usually you were kept in your place. For instance, next door to us there was the Elgoods and if my mother ever heard me say 'Hello Arthur,' or 'Hello Walter,' that was always 'Hello *Mr Elgood,* Agnes!' And they were just the sons. Or if the baker came round, that was always 'Mr Haydon' and 'Mr Taylor', never their Christian names.

If any of the children really were naughty we had a policeman who would come round and have a talk to them, but we never had any real trouble - there was no vandalism. The only thief in our family was our old dog. He used to bring my mother beautiful sweeping brushes home. People would say, 'Oh Mrs Cronk, I saw your Toby up Newmarket Road today,' or, 'I saw your Toby up Magdalen Street.' He would go after these ladies and they'd throw a brush at him to shoo him away. Well, he'd pick these up and bring them back. Mother had no end of brushes!

Agnes's Spicy Meat Loaf

Ingredients:
Either ¾ lb minced beef & ¼ lb sausage meat *or*
½ lb minced cooked chicken & ½ lb sausage meat;
1 medium onion finely chopped; 1 oz breadcrumbs; 1 egg;
1 level teaspoon mixed herbs or parsley; 1 tablespoon
tomato purée or ketchup; ½ teaspoon mixed spice;
salt and pepper; stock or water to mix.

Method:
Mix meats, onion and all dry ingredients in a bowl, add
purée or ketchup. Beat egg and add if necessary stock or
water to bind all together. Grease a loaf cake tin and pack
mixture in tin, pressing well down and smooth over top.
Cover with greaseproof paper or foil. Bake in oven, gas 4,
electric 350° F, for 1¼ - 1½ hours until meat begins to
shrink away from sides of tin. Serve hot with gravy or
cold with salad.

Mother's Lemon Cheese Tart

Ingredients:
Short pastry for case. Filling: 1½ oz of butter or margarine;
4 oz sugar, granulated; 1 egg; 1 lemon (rind and juice).

Method:
Line a sandwich tin with pastry. Soften butter or margarine
and gradually beat in the egg. Add sugar and the juice and
grated rind of the lemon. Pour into pastry case. Bake for
about 20 - 30 minutes at gas 5, electric 375° F.

'Here come the Vicar!'

My Mother was verger at St Etheldreda's Church in King Street, and just through the passageway from Big Ship Yard there was a Congregationalist chapel, in Sherbourne Place. I used to go to both, the church and the chapel, so I had two denominations! You didn't have any vicars or parsons in the chapel, they were all laymen - superintendents they were called - and it was very informal. We all went there when we were younger, and that used to be lovely, especially on anniversary days. We'd wear our white dresses, with little bunches of flowers, and perhaps we'd go to the main chapel in Princes Street. That was where the Colman family went, and they'd have big do's there. Sunday afternoons they always had a young men's bible class for all the youths of King Street and the surrounding area. If you went to these places every Sunday, you'd be able to go on the Sunday School treats. You'd go to as many as you could and have lovely school treats all through the year.

I started going to St Etheldreda's when I was about seven years old. Mother would take me along when they had weddings, and it was my job to collect all the confetti up afterwards. Then as soon as the wedding was over I would have to race down the church path and make sure the gates were closed - make sure there'd be no cattle running up. And when someone died I used to help Mother toll the funeral bells. There would be one toll of the bell for every year of their age, so when it was an elderly person she would say, 'Come on, you've got to come and help me.' They only had one bell - the other was cracked so they never used it - and you would go *pull*, then count *one, two, three, four, five, six, seven, eight, nine, ten,* and *pull!* Which was very tiring.

Mother was there for about forty-five years altogether. At first there was a Reverend Pierce, who retired, and then the Reverend Andrews came along, and he finished up at St Helen's Hospital. Then came the Reverend Selby-Strong. He was in the parish for thirty-odd years and after he came - while I was in the choir and everything - we used to have some jolly good times. He did a tremendous lot for the youngsters in those days, and he made it his business to make a nice churchyard so that people could visit. When he first went there it was terribly overgrown, very unkempt. He planted trees, and at night during the summer he'd get all the choir and everyone who belonged to his club to go gardening. Mind you, I don't know if very much gardening actually got done - the boys and girls used to lark about so much.

The Revd Selby-Strong with his group of players

He ran a club in the Parish Hall and each time you went you got a stamp, then at the end of the quarter you would get a medal. So of course you went - you really were keen. He used to put on plays and lantern shows in the hall, religious of course, and I remember one year he put on a pageant of the Christian year. The man who did all the signwriting for Steward and Paterson's was brought in to do the stage work, and his wife handled the costumes. Selby put each of us into groups - Christmas, Easter, Whitsun, all the way through the various feast days - and I was the Feast of the Circumcision. He used to teach us how to act, but I'm afraid that just started everyone giggling. He wasn't a very good-looking man, and he was very tall, so when he had to kneel down everybody used to laugh at him, because of his bulk alone. The pageant was a success though, and half the parish turned out to see it.

Another thing he organised was a badminton club, and he also used to take the boys and girls on evening rambles. We'd land right out at Keswick and then walk all the way round, or else he would hire a charabanc and take us down to the broads at Ranworth. We'd go on a Saturday afternoon and he would show us round the local church, then try to interest us in nature. He would always try to interest us in nature. He was a very good man really, but I don't think he ever really understood children, or the poorer class of people. He did try, he studied people very closely, but he wasn't able to mix very well. He didn't have the common touch.

He was a bachelor gentleman, very very big, and always had his hair cut like a monk. He was so highly educated that really I think he should have been in a monastery. A lot of people didn't like him because he couldn't bring himself down to their level; he didn't see a lot of humour in things. He would always shake hands, but he never said, 'How d'you do,' or anything, he just slipped his hand out. It was like shaking hands with an old codfish, it was so cold and slippery. One thing I know which used to get people's backs up was that he would always visit them at tea-time. I'm sure he didn't come to cadge anything, but that was always, 'Oh no, here come the vicar!'

It was a shame really, because he really did do his best. If he knew a child wanted a pair of boots he would buy them out of his own pocket, and in later years, during the bombing, as soon as the siren went he would get on his bicycle and come straight down to King Street. He lived on Grosvenor Road and he'd come down to visit all the shelters, to make sure his parishioners were alright. At the end he had diabetes and he had his leg off, but even then he would come down to officiate, in a wheelchair. He did try very hard.

Stuffed Herrings with Samphire

Ingredients:
4 herrings; 1 oz plain flour (seasoned); dripping.
Stuffing: 2 oz breadcrumbs; 1 tablespoon shredded suet;
1 tablespoon chopped parsley; 1 teaspoon mixed herbs;
1 egg; salt and pepper.

Method:
Stuffing: Make breadcrumbs and put in bowl with suet,
herbs and parsley. Season with salt and pepper. Beat egg
and add sufficient to bind all ingredients together.
Wash, scrape herrings. Trim off fins and tail. Split open.
Flatten and remove large bone and as many small bones as
possible. Score outside of fish in two or three places.
Spread stuffing inside. Roll up fish a rub over with
seasoned flour. Tie each herring securely with string. Place
in greased dish with a knob of dripping on top. Bake at
gas 5, electric 375°F for 20 minutes, basting occasionally.
Remove string. Serve on a hot dish garnished with parsley
and a sharp sauce.

Samphire
A sea herb rich in iron, still harvested along parts of our
Norfolk coast and sold by the pound in the local fish
shops. Samphire should be washed well and the roots cut
off. Wash again several times. Drop into a saucepan of
boiling water and cook until tender (about 20 minutes).
Drain and cover with vinegar. Eat same day or leave
overnight. Samphire is eaten with the fingers as one would
eat asparagus.

A Good Start in Life'

My brothers and sisters were a lot older than me. Sophie was the youngest and she was already ten when I was born. My eldest sister Bessie was married in 1926, and my brother Jack went to work in London when I was nine. He was steel-erecting for Boulton and Paul's. My brother Billy, well, he just left the house one Easter Monday and the next thing we knew he was a soldier. 'Cheerio Mother,' he said, 'I'll see you later.' And that was that. Of course, Mother had his dinner ready that lunchtime, and all afternoon she was sending me down the passage to see if he was on his way home. By the following day she was beginning to think the worst had happened, and then the message came that he'd joined the army - the Queen's Bays at Colchester. Because Mother wouldn't sign the papers for him he went and asked one of her cousins on Silver Road. Which left just me and Sophie at home with Mother.

Of course, I was at school by then. All the children in King Street began their schooling at Horn's Lane Infants, and when they got to seven they went up to the senior school at the top of the hill. My aunts used to go there, and so did my sisters, but in their time you stayed at Horn's Lane until you were fourteen. Then the rule changed, and when you were eleven they took you to another school. I went to Crook's Place, which is now the Bignold. It was a new school for us, but really you didn't feel out of place because all your friends went with you. Only girls of course - the boys were over the other side. I don't think we ever saw a boy, not in our school.

You were supposed to stay on until you were fourteen, but my birthday came during the holidays so I was able to leave at thirteen, in 1932 - I think I had all the knowledge I wanted by then! They were very strict in those days, but we were awfully fond of our teachers, and we were never rude to them. We also had a very good headmistress, a Miss Bill. I remember in one lesson I accidentally broke a pencil - I don't know what happened, but I was ever so interested in this pencil and it just went snap in my hands. The teacher sent me along to Miss Bill and I got a ruler six times across my knuckles, three on each hand, for being 'destructful'. She was very strict, but I don't think it did me any harm, because when you get to that age you need a little discipline.

I think they gave us a good start in life, preparing us for growing up. We had cookery lessons of course, how to make a meal out of nothing, and how to make bread, and they also taught us sewing and how to do the laundry. I suppose in a way they were teaching us how to be housewives, whereas at one time it would have been domestic service. All my aunts went into service, and so did my sisters to begin with. I wouldn't say it was a rebellion exactly, but the girls in my year weren't interested in service, not any more. I dare say there were one or two, because that was still a good life in some ways, but you didn't get a lot of money, and you didn't get much freedom. And that was the thing, freedom. The girls didn't want to be tied down, because in service you would be up early in the morning and then working all the day through, perhaps until half past ten at night if they were having a dinner party. I could have gone but my mother said, 'No, I don't want you in service, we'll find you another job.' There were a lot of factories then - boot factories, Colman's, Caley's, the big laundries - and for a time it was quite easy to get a job. I went to Harmer's clothing factory in St Andrew's to begin with, but at the end of my first week Mother told me there was a job going at Colman's, so I went there.

At that time, if you could get into Colman's you thought you were made. You knew you were more or less there for life, providing you didn't do anything silly. They were a very good firm to work for, and they really did try to look after their workforce. When I started at Harmer's I was on five shillings and sixpence, and that went up to seven and nine when I joined Colman's. Then they used to have an annual share-out, perhaps sixpence in the pound one year, tenpence in the pound the next. It all depended on how long you'd been there. I started off filling tins, then I went on to labelling, and then I was put on the spice mill, but wherever you went it smelt horrible. There was mustard, cayenne pepper, black pepper, white pepper, all the spices, and really that place was alive with people. There were so many floors. There was the oat mill, barley and groats, the printing works, the tin shop, and everybody had a uniform which went with their floor. In mustard we wore khaki-coloured overalls with a blue neck and blue cuffs made of a sort of drill cloth, very stiff, and it went down below your calf. In the tin shop I think they wore navy blue. You would take your overalls home and wash them at the weekend.

36

Every morning there would be a stream of people coming along King Street and down Carrow Hill to work at Colman's, and there used to be a steam hooter that went off at ten to eight, ten to one, and ten to two. You could hear it all over the city, and if the wind was blowing the right way you would even hear it in the country. It was a jolly good time-keeper, so if you were at the top of King Street when it blew you knew it was time to start running. My hours in the factory used to be from eight till six, but I wasn't there very long before I got a job in the kitchens. I had an aunt and a sister who worked in the kitchen at that time and if anybody was away they would send over to the firm for someone to help them. My aunt suggested that I should be sent for. And soon I was going backwards and forwards quite regularly, so when there was a vacancy I asked to be transferred.

**Colman's Luncheon Club girls - Agnes top left
Colman family house in background**

I worked in what was called the Staff Luncheon Club and I suppose we used to do about 120 lunches a day. It was never known as a canteen, always the Luncheon Club - that was all the clerks and accountants, the managers and directors and everything. The work-force had what was known as the Works Kitchen, and they had good meals in there and didn't pay a lot. Just down the hill as you came in the gates there was a doorway set in the wall, and the poor old

37

workers would go in there for their cup of cocoa and a wad of cake. But the staff lived off the fat of land, they really did. They had lovely large dining rooms and at each end there was a lounge, one for the ladies and one for the gentlemen. They used to retire to the lounges after their meal to sit and read, or smoke or whatever, and then a waitress would go round and serve them with coffee. We had about four waitresses, a couple of scullery maids, and then the cook, perhaps ten of us altogether, and the kitchen was quite a modern affair - you'd think it was very old fashioned now - but at that time it was considered a model kitchen.

I was there for about nine years altogether, and some of the time I worked in what was known as the experimental kitchen. It was housed in a cottage joined on to the works, and we used to test various new products in there. Then in the spring of 1941 I was engaged, and I left Colman's in October of that same year to get married. You didn't have long engagements during the war because you didn't know whether one or the other was going to get bumped off, but I'd known John since 1937, and we'd been courting since about 1939. He was in the Air Force then and one day he came home and said, 'If I get a leave in October, would you like to get married?' Well, you didn't do anything in those days without asking Mother first, and so I went to her. She said, 'Agnes, you get married for love. Don't get married because you want to leave work.' Which was a very wise saying. 'Oh no,' I said, 'I do love him!'

He was from Wells-on-Sea originally and he came to Norwich in 1936 to become an apprentice at Mann Egerton's. He lodged with an old road sweeper called Mr Postil at the top of King Street and one day Mother asked him if he'd like to come round, because he was all alone. We were already connected in a roundabout sort of way - my mother's sister-in-law by her first marriage was his mother's aunt-in-law! But I thought he was awful. 'Oh Mother,' I said, 'I don't like him at all!' But they say hate turns to love, and somewhere along the line we started going out together. Of course, we didn't have very much money - he was only getting about six shillings a week - so we used to go for long walks, perhaps down to Trowse, or we'd go up what was known as the seven footpaths and finish out at Arminghall. Then we'd have to be back at half past nine. There was no car and I never rode a bike, so I mean to say, that was true love, walking!

The war brought about a lot of changes because at one time you'd be courting for five years or more before you even thought of getting married. I had one aunt who was courting forty years, and she got married in 1934. I suppose that was so you could save up and get all your things together for your bottom drawer. A little old cottage wouldn't cost a lot - my aunt Gertie bought one at Weston for £40 - but even then you'd have to save hard for that. And with the war, you made the most of what you'd got, because you didn't know if you were going to lose each other.

Our wedding was in St Etheldreda's and in those days that would cost you seven shillings and sixpence, but the Reverend Selby Strong gave it to us as a wedding present. The organ was another five shillings, and that was a present from the organist, because I was in the choir. There were about fifty people and the whole reception cost my mother five pounds. Our wedding cake was a fruitcake, and sugar was scarce so we didn't have icing, just rice paper. You had to scheme during the war, and if your mother could scheme then you lived fairly well. My sister worked in a grocer's on Prince of Wales Road, so we never went short of butter, and for weddings people would rally round to provide clothing coupons. My dress cost me £3 from Bonds, and I had an underskirt made out of parachute silk which John brought home from the Air Force.

Once we were married, John was posted all over the country. We lived in Hunstanton for a while, and then I went with him to Wick in Scotland, where we stayed for about two years until finally they sent him abroad. We didn't know where he was being sent, but it turned out to be Burma, after which I didn't see him again until the end of the Japanese war. I came back to Norwich when he went overseas, and that's when I got the job at Carrow Abbey, looking after the Miss Colmans. So I ended up in service after all.

Miss Helen's Chicken Casserole

Ingredients:
1 chicken or 4 chicken joints; 4 shallots (chopped);
3 tomatoes (chopped); 3 tablespoons cooking oil;
6 peppercorns; 1 oz plain flour; 1 oz margarine or butter;
stock or gravy; salt; tomatoes and
hard-boiled eggs for garnishing.

Method:
Joint chicken or quarter if whole, heat oil in casserole and
lay in chicken joints. Cook until golden brown, gas 5-6,
electric 375°- 400°F. Stir in shallots and place back in
oven for a few minutes longer, then add tomatoes,
peppercorn, stock or gravy, salt to taste. Place casserole
back in oven. Cook until chicken is tender. Melt margarine
in a saucepan, stir in flour and let it colour without
burning. Add sufficient liquid from casserole to make a
thick sauce. Arrange chicken joints on a hot dish and cover
with sauce. Garnish with sliced tomatoes and sliced
hard-boiled eggs.

Miss Stancombe's Autumn Pudding

Ingredients:
4 oz plain flour; 4 oz suet; 3 oz soft brown sugar;
2 oz breadcrumbs; 8 oz dried fruit; 2 eggs;
½ teaspoon bicarbonate soda; ½ teaspoon mixed spice;
3 tablespoons milk.

Method:
Mix dry ingredients together. Dissolve bicarbonate in milk.
Beat eggs. Stir into dry ingredients with milk and
bicarbonate. Turn into a greased 1½ pint basin. Cover with
greaseproof paper or foil and steam for 2½ hours.
Serve with a sweet sauce.

'We're in the Hall!'

Years before the war Carrow Abbey used to be opened on Sundays for people to come and look around. The Abbey belonged to Mr and Mrs Stuart, and really that was a beautiful place. One of the Colman daughters, Laura, had married into the Stuart family, and that was where she lived. Then after she and her husband died, Miss Helen and Miss Ethel Colman went to live there.

They were very nice ladies, maiden ladies, but they were in their eighties by the time I worked for them, and they still sort of lived in the Victorian era. They dressed in a late-Victorian style - full skirts and high waists, hats perched on top of their heads - and they used to treat me as though I was the same age. They would ask me if I remembered things that happened before I was born, and of course the other servants were all getting on in years too.

Laura the housemaid was in her seventies, and there was a lovely old boy called Mr Hubbard who used to come and rake out the donkey stove on Mondays and Fridays, and he was well over seventy. Three or four times a week we had old Mrs Bunting come in to flick a duster about, and there was one very old lady who used to do all the hard scrubbing on Fridays. She came down from Hall Road and she was in her nineties! We had a lot of gardeners - no end of gardeners when I was there - and they were all quite elderly as well. They also had a permanent companion, a lovely lady called Miss Palmer. She was a cousin of the family and did all their secretarial duties. She may have got a small salary, but that was her home, and she lived solely at Carrow Abbey. We were the only two who lived in. Laura, the housemaid, should have lived in, but the Abbey was hit by a bomb shortly before I came and she was too frightened to stay. All the staff were, myself included, but I thought, 'Well, I'm here now and that's that.' And of course, being so near King Street I could get away every day to see Mother.

In the evenings we would go to bed early, and I had to sleep in what was known as the Servants' Hall. The ladies refused to go upstairs - they slept in the dining room - and they had these long basket beds which were kept outside in the sunhouse. Every evening I would have to wheel these beds out across the lawn and bring them inside. All through the summer they had hot water bottles which it was my job to fill, and they also had a big old Persian cat called Tinker who used to be put out at nine o'clock. Well, of course that'd be a job to find him. Sometimes he wouldn't come in, so poor Miss Helen would have to go and call him in before we could go to bed. Then if there were any sirens during the night I would have to go and wake the ladies up and help them to get dressed, and we would sit in what was known as the Tiled Hall. The kitchens led off from there, and the storeroom and everything, and they thought that if ever a bomb dropped on the abbey it would have three floors to come through first, so they'd be safe. There was a phone at the end of this hall, and I always remember we used to have to sit around it - they seemed to think that if ever a bomb dropped they would be able to telephone out and say, 'We're in the hall!' They were very very nervous, but really they weren't in a safe place at all, not where we sat.

In the morning I'd get up at about seven and come down to the kitchen to put the stove on, the old donkey stove - a combustion stove, what they called a 'tortoise' - and that used to heat all the water. If it was a Monday or a Friday I would have to wait for Mr Hubbard to come in and rake it all out, because the ladies always looked to have their bath on those nights, and of course I'd have to have my bath on those nights too. Then I would get their breakfast, and I always had to grind the coffee, because they lived very frugally. For breakfast they would have toast, or perhaps a boiled egg - not many eggs, because they were rationed. I had to ration all their marmalade and butter and sugar. They lived by their rations; they solely lived on them, my ration of butter for instance had to be in a separate dish from theirs. We had a dish each.

Of course, they did live fairly well because, unbeknown to them, the manageress in the Carrow kitchen - Miss Stancombe - used to help me out with little bits and pieces. If they had known they wouldn't have eaten it, because one day they happened to be in the kitchen when Miss Stancombe sent a cake over, and it was sent straight back. And the ladies, unlike us, saved every bit of string and every bit of brown paper. They were very careful.

As soon as breakfast was over I would have to clear the table and start preparing lunch. I used to have to make a 3 lb chicken last a week. I remember the second day I was there I roasted a chicken and Miss Palmer said to me, 'Do as you like with the chicken, they like it roasted.' So I said, 'Alright.' Well, they had a lovely big garden and there was no stint on any of the vegetables, everything in season. So of course I cooked the old bird and sent it in with plenty of vegetables, and then later I took the sweet through and cleared the table. 'Well,' I thought, 'they haven't eaten much of that chicken,' and I called to the housemaid Laura. 'Come on Laura,' I said, 'that's time for our lunch!' I made us a Yorkshire pudding and carved up the bird and we had that with about four vegetables. 'Oh,' said Laura, 'I haven't had a lunch like this in years.' 'Well,' I said, 'that's how you're going to live now that I'm here, because I believe in good living!'

The following morning they all went off to Princes Street Chapel and Miss Palmer came to me and said, 'We'll have the cold chicken today, and do some potatoes and vegetables.' I had no choice. I sent the old bird through - what was left of it - and it come back at once, sort of *flew* out. 'Oh,' said Miss Palmer, 'the ladies *are* angry!' Well, there were no refrigerators then, so I said, 'Why? Has the chicken gone off?' 'No!' she said. 'You must *never* touch the chicken. If *they* have chicken you must have sausages. You don't eat their chicken!' So I learned my lesson, that old chicken had to last till the Friday. Mind you, their appetite wasn't that great because they were so elderly. They didn't take a lot of looking after really.

Laura always did the tea, so I had a free afternoon till the next meal was served at night. The ladies had a very nice car and sometimes they would go out, but not very often, they were too aged by then. They were very interested in the Oxford Movement, which was connected with the Princes Street Chapel, and they had quite a lot of literature on that. They were very ardent Princes Street people, and used to do lots of things for the chapel. They always interested themselves in something - perhaps it would be bits and pieces of history about the factory, or maybe the garden. On Fridays for instance, they would have all the pot-plants brought in from the garden and arranged around the hall, which had a wonderful picture called 'Dante's Dream of Beatrice', but of course most of their valuable paintings were put into safe hiding during the war because of the bombing.

In the evenings there wasn't really anything much to do. They did have a wireless, but it would only be on for the news, nothing else. They used to sit and read quite a lot, and they also used to talk to me about the old days. Miss Ethel had been the Lord Mayor of Norwich once, in 1926, and at one time they'd had a wherry called the Hathor, which was named after the place in Egypt where Jeremiah Colman's son died. They liked to tell me about that, but it was passing the time really, because you could see they were nervous in case the bombers came over. They were very sad times for people, very worrying times. And of course, there was a terrible lot of bombing around King Street.

Aunt Muriel's Rhubarb Flan

Ingredients:
1 lb rhubarb; 1 egg; short pastry enough to line a tart plate; sugar;
1 oz sultanas or currants.

Method:
Cut rhubarb into small pieces. Cook in saucepan without any sugar and just enough water to prevent pan from burning. When cooked, strain off juice and leave fruit in a bowl to cool. Line open tart plate with pastry. Beat egg and add to rhubarb with dried fruit and sugar to taste. Stir until well mixed. Pour into pastry case. Cut pastry trimmings into strips and lay lattice wise across mixture. Bake at gas 5, electric 375°F until pastry is cooked and mixture set.

'Whatever is going on?'

By 1938 Mother had moved round the corner from Ship Yard to Mariner's Lane, and that's where we were when the bombing began. When the war started of course I was still working at Colman's factory, and I think it was the following week that some bombs dropped on Mousehold. My brother Billy was home on leave then, so there was Billy, my mother and I, all sitting round the table. Now Sunday night we had winkles for tea because the fishermen used to come round that morning selling them from a headbasket - sometimes that would be shrimps, or bloaters, whatever was in season. You'd buy a pint and usually it was the man of the house who got the most. For the children they were a treat because each winkle had a little cap which you could take off and put on your face as a beauty spot. Well, this Sunday we were having winkles, tinned pears and custard, and there was some cake - I can see the table now - when all of a sudden there was this terrible explosion. It rocked the whole house, and I don't know what happened but Billy flew up from the table and his knee caught the edge. All the winkles went flying up in the air and came raining back on top of us. We were absolutely flummoxed. Never experienced anything like it. We all laid on the floor, covered in winkles!

Not long after that a bomb exploded in Compass Street, I remember we had my aunt from Ber Street staying with us, and Mrs Goodson the pork butcher's wife. Mr Goodson had died by then and so she used to sleep at our house because she was frightened of being on her own. I was sleeping in Mother's bed, Billy was in the little back bedroom, and it was early morning - very light because it was summer. All of a sudden I heard this terrible crash. I opened the windows and, as I opened them, I could see all the houses in Compass Street going up in the air. And my brother kept some rabbits in a shed, and oh, they were screaming something dreadful! Billy shouted, 'Get downstairs!' and we all scrambled to the kitchen in our nightclothes and laid in a lump on the floor - three ladies, Billy and I - and that little old kitchen was hardly six feet long. Then after a little while we knew the bombing was over, and we went out to have a look. We were very lucky - our windows were out, but I think there were about three houses completely destroyed. It was

45

Agnes's Christmas Cake

Ingredients:
4 oz plain flour; 4 oz self-raising flour; 8 oz dark brown sugar; 8 oz butter; 4 eggs; 8 oz currants; 12 oz sultanas; 12 oz raisins; 4 oz cherries; 4 oz peel; 1 teaspoon of mixed spice; ½ teaspoon nutmeg.

Method:
Wash and well dry fruit. Chop cherries. Cream together butter and sugar. Beat in eggs one at a time then lightly fold in flour and spices. Add fruit, cherries and peel. Mix thoroughly. Grease and double line with greaseproof paper a 7" or 8" cake tin. Put mixture in tin and make small well in middle. Bake for 1½ hours on middle shelf in oven preheated to gas 2, electric 300°F. Turn heat down to gas 1, electric 275°F and cook for a further 3 hours. If no icing is required cover top of cake with almond halves before baking.

Almond Paste

Ingredients:
4 oz ground almonds; 4 oz caster sugar; 1 egg yolk; few drops of almond essence.

Method:
Mix dry ingredients together. Add enough egg yolk to make a firm mixture. Knead thoroughly. This is enough to cover the top of the Christmas cake. Spread top of cake with apricot jam. Roll out almond paste to cover top of cake. Press on to cake and roll lightly with rolling pin until level. Keep in airtight tin until ready for icing.

dreadful, and the smell when the bombs went off was something really awful.

One of the first siren suits.

They built a brick shelter in Compass Street after that and we used to go in there when there was a raid on. It was quite long; the lights were all dimmed, and at one end there was an old bin for a toilet. They were dangerous things really, but I suppose you needed to be underground if you really wanted to be safe. I remember there was one particular lady who always used to keep us amused. She didn't mean to of course, but as soon as she got in this shelter she would have to go to the toilet. 'There she goes!' someone would say, or if she sat there for a little while first, 'She'll be on there in a minute!' There was a lot of humour in the shelters, but I suppose there had to be, because you didn't know how long you'd be waiting for the all clear. One night in particular there was a *terrible* explosion - they dropped two landmines on Lakenham pool - and I remember as I came out of there I said to my mother, 'I don't think I can bear this any longer!' 'Well,' she said, 'you'll just have to. You'll have to be like other people and put up with it.' I suppose the mothers had already been through one war and they knew a little of what to expect.

Later on I think it was decided that it would be best if you packed a suitcase of clothes for when the sirens went. My sister was living with us then, and she had her little girl with her. She had one of the first siren suits that came out for children, and I can see it now, a little brown thing with fur round the hood. She used to be zipped up in her nightclothes, nice and warm. So as soon as the sirens went Sophie would take care of the baby, and I'd have to run down the shelter with three suitcases. Mother would be getting her corsets on. If a bomb had then been dropping on the house Mother would have said, 'I must get my corsets on!' One night they were pretty near and I can remember Sophie saying, 'Oh blow your corsets!' But no, she had to have them on - I think people of her age thought it was rather disgusting if you went out of the house without them. And by that time of course it wasn't sufficient to sit in the shelters on benches, they had to have their deckchairs, so as soon as I'd taken the suitcases I'd have to run back and fetch the deckchairs, all whilst the planes were coming over. We'd eventually get in there, and of course we'd sit there until the All Clear went, perhaps until the next morning.

They had the blackout then and you weren't allowed to show a single chink of light through your windows. You daren't open your door with a light on, even a cigarette light, because they said it could be seen from the sky. You had to be so careful. A lot of people put up wooden shutters and I can remember my mother made some black curtains. One time, I couldn't find my way out of the house. That was so stupid! I'd lived in it all those years, but I just couldn't find the door because it was pitch black and you daren't put a light on.

One weekend I remember Mother went to stay in the country with one of my aunts, and she left Sophie and I behind with the baby. Well, there was this terrible crash, and of course we couldn't see out. So Sophie said to me, 'Come on, we'll get in the cupboard.' They did say that was the best place to go, either under a table or in a cupboard under the stairs. Our cupboard was then full of saucepans and we climbed in there, suitcases, baby and all. It wasn't very big, but we were quite comfortable, so we just sat and waited for the All Clear to go. It got to three o'clock in the morning and we still hadn't heard anything. 'That's funny,' my sister said, 'there's not been any planes over. And there's been no All Clear. Whatever is going on?' Well, we sat there a little while longer and then she said, 'Look, you keep still, I'm going to have a look out the front door.' So she opened the door and peeped out and there was a policeman coming by, wheeling his bike. 'Oh,' she said, 'whenever is this raid going to be over!' 'There ain't been no raid,' he said, 'that was a thunder storm!' But that's how you were, you were so keyed up for the bombs falling!

48

In the early part of the war there were five or six girls killed onCarrow Hill. They'd just then left off from Colman's. It was about five o'clock and this plane went over and dropped a stick of bombs on them. In another raid they went over to Boulton and Paul's and dropped a stick on the paint department. Later on Carrow Works got hit and I remember I was in Magdalen Street. My sister-in-law was going to get married that June and we were on our way up to Sprowston to borrow a veil for her head-dress. Half-way down Magdalen Street there was this terrific explosion - no sirens or anything - and of course everyone was screaming 'Bombs! Bombs! Bombs!' So we just dived into this pub and when the All Clear went we hurried back to King Street. That was a very sad do. We knew one of the men who was killed, and there was a lovely new sweet shop called Yallops nearly opposite Carrow Bridge - it had just opened and was really swishy, mirrors all round the walls and flowers in the window - and that was totally bombed out, completely taken down. Then there was a little row of houses close by called Cinder Oven Row, and that was all bombed.

Really, that was the beginning of the end for King Street, the bombing. I remember the end of the European war. My sister and I went up the City Hall. That was a marvellous night. There was only a faint breeze, but it was strong enough to blow the flag out on City Hall. It was just blowing, and then they put the searchlight on it. Of course, my husband was still out in Burma, they were still fighting out there, but that was a wonderful feeling and everyone was so happy. We've lost that wartime spirit. It's a shame there has to be something awful happen to make people friendly like that. John eventually landed in England on Christmas night when the Burma war had finished. I'd just been down the lane to lock up the church, and I can still see him now, coming around the church corner in his demob suit. And oh, I was so pleased to see him. But I was even more pleased about two weeks later when his kit arrived home - there were tins of salmon, boxes of tea, packets of Persil! All from Bombay. We hadn't seen anything like it. That was marvellous!

Something on the Cards

The bombing did a lot of damage to King Street, and then, after the war, everything changed completely. We knew something was on the cards because we had various people coming round with clipboards, and gradually that got to be known that they were going to clear the whole area. They were building all the estates then and people were being rehoused. The youngsters were getting married and coming straight on to the estates, whereas at one time they'd try to find a little cottage near to their mother. And once they moved someone out they boarded the house up rather than move new people in. That became a very dejected area. The little shops started to fade out because there wasn't the custom, and then Watney's began pulling the brewery all about, which altered things completely.

The city planners could be very ruthless, and I think they pulled down a lot of places which should never have been pulled down, but I suppose they were young men and they wanted to get on, and that was a new beginning for everyone. Some of the houses that did come down were in a very bad state, so that was for the best because people were being given decent homes to live in. But the main thing that was lost was neighbourliness. Normandy Tower was built more or less where we used to live in Mariner's Lane, and that house had been in my mother's family for seventy-odd years.

She was the last one to move from there I think. I remember we had to go up to City Hall because it was infested with rats - it was dreadful. But that was still a big wrench to leave. Her roots were well and truly established, and of course, she had to leave her church. The Reverend Selby Strong had died by then, and so the bishop closed the church down. I dare say a lot of the old dears who moved out died of broken hearts nearly. When you begin your life in the same house and practically end it there, then they haul you out and put you somewhere else - it's a job to get used to. Mother eventually got a place in Hobart's Square, but she never did like it. She didn't have a back door and she used to complain that she felt all closed in. It was quite a nice little flat, but for the old people the change was very hard to accept, especially when they'd been living in somewhere like King Street.

They were very good days when I was there - hard days I know, but sometimes I think I'd like those days back. When you went along everybody you saw would say, 'Hello, how are you?' Whereas today you could go out and no one would say a word to you, they don't want to. I'm glad I was born in King Street, I'll say that. I had a very happy childhood. They were lovely days and I'm very glad I knew them.

The wedding of Agnes to John Davey.